BASIC ILLUSTRATED
Animal Tracks

Second Edition

Jonathan and Roseann Hanson

FALCON GUIDES

GUILFORD, CONNECTICUT
HELENA, MONTANA

An imprint of Rowman & Littlefield
Falcon and FalconGuides are registered trademarks and Make Adventure Your Story is a trademark of Rowman & Littlefield.

Distributed by NATIONAL BOOK NETWORK

Copyright © 2016 by Rowman & Littlefield
A previous edition of this book was published by Globe Pequot Press in 2001.

Maps © Rowman & Littlefield

Track illustrations on pp. 29, 35, 47, 53, 59, 63, 65, 73, 77, and 85 by Roseann and Jonathan Hanson. All other track illustrations by Lisa Reneson, based on original submissions from Roseann and Jonathan Hanson.

Photos on pp. vi, x, 3–5, 8–15, 18, 88–95, and 97 by Roseann and Jonathan Hanson. Photos on pp. 20–86 by Thinkstock.com, except western spotted skunk on p. 46 courtesy of Axle Canyon Ecological Preserve.

British Library Cataloguing-in-Publication Information available

Library of Congress Cataloging in Publication Data available

ISBN 978-1-4930-1717-1 (paperback)
ISBN 978-1-4930-1718-8 (e-book)

∞™ The paper used in this publication meets the minimum requirements of American National Standard for Information Sciences—Permanence of Paper for Printed Library Materials, ANSI/NISO Z39.48-1992.

CONTENTS

INTRODUCTION

Imagine, for a moment, that instead of being a modern, pinnacle-of-evolution *Homo sapiens*, you are a proto mammal living in the early Jurassic Period, around 200 million years ago. Pinnacle of evolution, not so much: You're about the size of a shrew, and your main goal in life is to avoid being either eaten or inadvertently stomped flat by a dinosaur several thousand times your weight. At this point you aren't even any smarter than those things. So how do you survive? Simple—you go nocturnal, an adaptation made easy by your warm-blooded physiology.

Flash forward to the present. The dinosaurs are gone; the largest and meanest and smartest land animals are all mammals. And yet about 70 percent of all mammal species remain nocturnal, doing most if not all their moving, hunting, grazing, playing, and mating when you're asleep. Sure, you'll see the odd squirrel or deer or coyote out in daylight, but there's an entire mammalian world that is otherwise hidden.

Hidden, that is, unless you know a bit about tracking and reading sign, in which case you can peek into that world like a naturalist Sherlock Holmes and uncover fascinating details about the animals whose paths you are crossing—sometimes only hours after they were there.

Picture a grassy meadow with a small stream running across one side, tall trees and a thicket of berry bushes marking its sinuous path. It's midmorning, the sun is warm, and there are a few birds chirping, but otherwise it's perfectly still, not an animal in sight. A scene that may seem devoid of wildlife, however, remains so only to the uninitiated. If you know just a little bit about finding and reading animal footprints and evidence of their feeding and communication, you'll discover that this "empty" meadow is actually the busiest place around—a veritable Serengeti of animal activity. Bear tracks around the berry bushes show where a female black bear ate a snack; bits of crayfish shells on the streambank and little hand-like prints tell of a raccoon's breakfast; a scraped-up area the size of a dinner plate, with round pellets scattered around it, marks a cottontail's favorite dust bath; a shredded shrub is the victim of a young white-tailed buck's pre-rut jousting as he rubs the shedding velvet from his antlers; and a long set of big-cat prints walking down the meadow trail tells of a mountain lion's search for supper.

You don't have to be a grizzled old woodsman or come from a long line of Native American trackers to enjoy animal tracking or to do it well. It's not a mystical art. All you need are three well-developed skills, which we all have and can improve: observation, patience, and awareness.

Observation

Your best tool is your ability to observe a track scene and take in all the clues left by the animal—not just the physical tracks, but also details such as which way the animal was going, if the animal veered off a trail to one side or the other briefly, if it was alone or in a group, if it walked down the middle of the trail or just darted across, and if it left any other marks like scratchings or piles of scat. Each of these clues can be used to identify the animal that made the track, but you need to observe carefully as well as truthfully: It's easy to turn a track or scene into what you'd like it to be rather than what it is. Don't forget to notice physical and geographic details: habitat, topography, weather, season, and so on. Stay quiet, too—it helps concentration.

Patience

Slowing down is actually the hardest tracking skill for most people to develop. In order to practice tracking well, you need to take lots of time to observe the scene and do so slowly and methodically, from all angles (get down on your hands and knees, too). It's almost a kind of meditation. Some practitioners get into the mind or even the physical aspect of the animal: If you were a bear walking down this trail, where would you walk, what would you eat, where would you be going and when?

Awareness

Awareness of your natural surroundings is a skill that comes only with study and practice. If you are going to be a successful tracker, you need to learn about your surroundings—the plants, the animals, the weather, the seasons—what happens when, which creatures are active when, what blooms or fruits when. Learn the life histories of the animals, their eating and traveling and mating habits. This is nature awareness. It's incredibly fulfilling, and it will make you a superb tracker because you'll know that, for example, kit foxes are almost strictly carnivores—kangaroo rats are their favorite prey—and live in the desert. You won't find them in mountain canyons, where you're more likely to find their relative the gray fox.

Getting Started

This book, as its title implies, is intended as an introduction to the art and science of tracking. You'll eventually want other field guides in addition to this one: books about mammal (or bird or reptile) identification, with range maps and life history information. An advanced tracking book will be useful as well, such as Olaus J. Murie's *Animal Tracks*—a remarkable compendium of information about the natural history and tracking of North American mammals, birds, reptiles, and insects. Plant books are useful for identifying plants used by animals you are tracking. Look also for nature guides to your region.

Use this book as a tool to get started enjoying the art of tracking. Develop your three skills—observation, patience, and awareness—and build your library of notes on the tracks in your ecosystem. We provide a starting point for learning about the animals, but you'll no doubt want to delve further with other sources of natural history information. Finally, we provide information on how to use animal tracking in conservation projects, so that future generations will have as much fun as we do discovering the world of animal tracking.

Mountain lions are normally solitary animals, so it's unusual to find a paired set of tracks. Note how well the prints show up in this late afternoon light.

1 Tracking—Science or Art?

It's both, of course. There are specific techniques that will help you maximize your success in finding and deciphering tracks and sign, but the more creative you are in your approach to the science, the more you'll get out of it. Let's look at technique first.

When to Track

It makes sense that if you want to decipher the activities of nocturnal animals, the best time to do it is as soon as possible after those animals have been active, in the early morning, before the tracks can be blurred by wind or trampled over by humans. But there's an even bigger advantage to tracking early in the morning: When the sun is low in the sky, it casts a shadow into tracks that makes them pop out of the background—*as long as you are looking toward the sun*. Do an experiment—find some soft dirt early on a sunny morning and plant one of your own footprints in it. Walk 10 feet or so toward the sun and look back at your track. Now walk to the other side of it, so the sun is shining into the track and into your face. See how the shadow makes the print jump out? Walking toward the sun is one of the most effective techniques you can use to spot tracks. If you have to walk away from the sun while looking, be sure to turn around every few feet and check back along your path. We've lost count of how many times we've found tracks that were virtually invisible with the sun behind us, but which became obvious once we looked the other way.

Late afternoon light is just as effective for highlighting tracks, although they might be a bit more indistinct after a day of breeze or other traffic. But what if the only time you can be out is at midday? The trick is to carry a mirror about the size of a large track (we use 4- by 5-inch signaling mirrors because they're sturdy enough to carry in a back pocket). If you spot something that looks like a print but has no definition, try this: Squat down and shade the track with your body, then use the mirror to shine reflected sunlight on the track from just a foot or so off the ground. What you're doing in essence is creating slanting early morning light, and you'll be surprised at how effective it is. We once positively identified mountain lion tracks along an important wildlife movement corridor with just this trick. On overcast days a good flashlight can produce similar results.

Where to Track

You can track anywhere, but hiking trails and dirt roads are used by many animals as it is just as easy for them to travel that way as it is for humans. We once tracked a mountain lion for over 4 miles as she walked straight down a canyon road after sauntering past our house. Also, the substrate of trails and dirt roads is continuously pulverized, making it softer and better able to register clear tracks. Other excellent places to look for tracks include the banks of streams and ponds, where mud preserves tracks well. A field after a fresh snowfall can be a virtual encyclopedia of tracks.

Some notes on substrates:

- A thin layer of fine dirt over a firm underlayer (such as that well-traveled dirt road) is superb for registering a perfect track imprint. However, a crisp track in fine dirt is very susceptible to wind blurring—not to mention getting destroyed completely if a vehicle drives over it. It's best to check dirt roads early in the morning.

- Fairly firm mud can also provide an excellent canvas for tracks, and will retain a clear image as it hardens. Very soft mud, however, can distort tracks wildly, creating what appears to be a huge imprint as the soft material is pushed up and away from the animal's foot as it sinks into the ooze. Our favorite plaster cast is one Jonathan managed to get home intact from Zambia. He was at a camp in the Luangwa Valley and had a bucket-style shower in his tent after a day of hiking. The water ran out under the canvas—and the next morning he found an enormous male lion track perfectly placed in the center of it.

- Coarse sand takes tracks poorly—it's obvious there is a print there, but many times there is zero detail, and the depression could just as easily be a coyote or a deer.

- Forest soils are theoretically good for tracking; unfortunately they're usually covered by a carpet of leaves. You need to search for clearings or trails, where the leaves tend to be scuffed away.

- Snow is a highly variable substrate for tracking. New powder will clearly indicate that an animal has passed, but detail might be completely lacking. On the other hand, old crusted snow might not show any sign at all that a good-sized animal has walked over it. A thin layer of slightly wet snow is excellent for registering clear tracks, as is frozen older snow with a thin new layer on top.

A cougar track in firm mud remains clear after the substrate has dried.

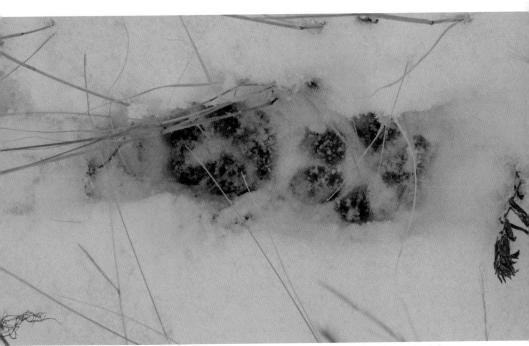

These coyote tracks show up well in a light snowfall. Note the obvious X in the print on the right.

How to Track

As you move along a trail looking for prints, especially early in the morning, it's important not to destroy a track set you might not yet have noticed. Don't walk in the middle of the trail where tracks are most likely to show. You should walk off on the edge of the trail (or in the harder center of a two-track road), where prints would not be as likely to register and walking over them will not do so much harm. Go slowly—tracking is rarely an aerobic exercise!

Once you spot a track, it's natural to get excited and immediately cluster around with your companions to examine it. Don't. Stop where you are (and tell everyone else to stop) and see if you can spot other prints. Often the first track you see will not be the clearest one in a string, and if you trample others you could ruin your chances for getting positive identification or finding out anything else about the animal. We like to paraphrase an old aphorism to remind us not to rush things: "Don't just do

Even in flat light this line of cougar tracks shows up well in slightly damp sand, which darkens as it is compressed. Note how well the three-lobed metacarpal and metatarsal pads show up.

something; stand there." If you can't see any other tracks, go ahead and move closer to the one you spotted, keeping an eye out for others—there almost always will be others. Now you can determine the path of the animal and the direction of travel, and look for the clearest tracks to make an identification.

What Else to Consider

Successful tracking doesn't involve simply identifying prints with a picture. The more knowledge you have of the natural history of the animal and of your area, the more effective you'll be.

Obviously the most basic thing to consider once you think you've identified a track is whether or not you are in that animal's known range. For example, if you find a bear track in the coastal mountains of southern California, it is far, far more likely to have been made by a black bear than a grizzly. Habitat within that known range is important as well. A fox track in the mountainous oak woodlands in southern Arizona is much more likely to have been made by a gray fox than a kit fox. Both can be found in that part of the state, but the kit fox inhabits low deserts.

Keep in mind geographic differences in size. Animals in warm southern climates are usually smaller than the same species in the northern parts of the range. A desert coyote might weigh 20 or 25 pounds; one from a northern forest could be close to twice that, with a corresponding difference in track measurements. This book is intended as a general guide; local track cards or books for your own area can offer specifics on what track sizes to expect.

Lastly, although it might sound silly: Don't forget to look around for real live animals as you track! Twice that we can remember, we had been following a set of tracks and looked up to see the animal that made them staring at us with intense curiosity. Another incident was a bit more startling. We were on our way home to the remote house we were caretaking on a wildlife refuge when we saw fresh drag marks across the dirt road, where some predator had pulled a kill under cover. I stayed to investigate while Roseann drove

Body (and track) size in most mammal species increases the farther north they are found. This is a wolf print from north of the Arctic Circle. A print from a Mexican wolf in Arizona would be noticeably smaller.

the mile to the house to retrieve a camera. I found a white-tailed deer carcass under a mesquite tree, still warm, and obvious signs of a mountain lion. Confident the cat would have vacated the area as soon as our vehicle showed up, I began crawling under the brush to find more sign. On my hands and knees, I looked up to see the lion crouched under a shrub not 15 feet away. The instant our eyes met, she turned and simply vanished, but it took awhile for my pulse to settle down.

2 Identifying Tracks

Definitions

Just in case you've been watching too many movies, we should start with a dose of reality: Don't expect that after reading this book you'll be able to glance down at a track and say sagely to nearby admirers, "Ah, a female cougar, four years old. Passed by about two and a half hours ago. She'd just fed on a deer carcass. And she's limping."

With that said, there is often an extraordinary amount of information that can be deduced from a track or a set of tracks—if you know what to look for and take your time looking for it. Depending on the condition of the print and whether it is repeated, you might be able to identify the species of the animal, roughly how long ago it passed, if it is an adult or juvenile, male or female, and whether it was walking, running—or perhaps stalking.

You're about to learn how tracks are made and how to deduce information from them, but first you need to be familiar with some terms. (Note that throughout the book we use the terms "track" and "print" interchangeably.)

Pad: Pads are what make the track in animals such as cats and dogs. You usually see the prints from the toe pads and the big pad behind the toes. That big pad is called the palmar or metacarpal pad if it is a front foot print; if a rear foot print it is called the plantar or metatarsal pad. To remember metacarpal and metatarsal, recall that wrist problems caused by repetitive stress are often diagnosed as carpal tunnel syndrome; your wrists are attached to what would be your front feet if you still went on all fours. We often just call the big pad "the big pad" if we cannot immediately determine if the track is a front or rear foot!

Hoof: Hoofed animals (ungulates) leave a much different print, either from a single hoof in animals such as horses or zebras (order Perissodactyla), or a double hoof in animals such as cows, deer, elk, pigs, and camels (order Artiodactyla). (Rhinos, also perissodactyls, have three hooves.) The double hoof in a deer is actually its highly modified third and fourth toes; a horse walks entirely on a modified third toe.

True track: Obtaining an accurate measurement of a track is critical to proper identification of species, and it can sometimes help determine sex and age. When you measure a track, you attempt to measure the actual size of the foot that left it, not the larger track created by the displaced soil. Study the track carefully and measure only the bottom of its plane (imagine the animal's foot making the track and pushing dirt out of the way, and measure only the part that represents the foot). In some substrates—for example, a thin layer of dirt over rock—this is easy. In others—especially mud—it can be very difficult, as the weight of the animal will push a great deal of material up and out of the actual track.

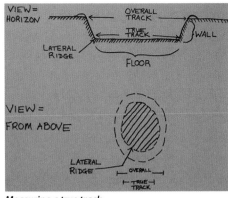

Measuring a true track.

Overall length and width: The overall size of the track is crucial to proper species identification, and in some cases can help you determine sex as well. To determine overall length, hold your ruler just above the track (so you don't disturb it) along the direction of travel—don't skew the measurement by holding the ruler diagonally. Move it back and forth until you find the longest measurement. For example, in

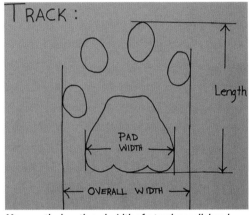

Measure the length and width of a track parallel and perpendicular with the direction of travel.

most cats, which have a leading toe, you'll want to measure from the back of the big pad to the end of that toe. Do the same for width, holding the ruler perpendicular to the line of travel. Remember to measure the true track and not the displaced substrate.

Pad length and width: For some of the larger mammals, measurements of the larger (metacarpal or metatarsal) pads can be useful for identification. Proceed as above, with your ruler along or perpendicular to the line of travel.

Stride: This is the length of each step the animal makes. It can be measured from any foot: from the print of one front paw to the next print of the same paw, or a hind paw. It doesn't matter whether you measure from the toe to the toe, or the rear of the print to the rear, as long as it's consistent. We won't deal much with stride measurements here, but some advanced tracking books do.

Straddle: This is the distance between each foot left to right, measured from inside edge to inside edge. This book does not go into straddle measurements, which vary widely, but other books do provide that information.

Trail: A track trail is simply a line of tracks from a single animal.

Double register: Both carnivores and their prey sometimes walk by placing their hind feet in the same spot where they placed their front feet, thus diminishing the chance they will make noise when stalking—or attempting to avoid being stalked. Reading these tracks can be difficult, because the hind-foot track mixes with that of the front.

Gait: This is the arrangement that all the tracks (front and hind, left and right) make in different modes or speeds of travel, such as walking, loping, bounding, stalking, or diagonal trotting.

This mountain lion print is an example of a double register. Note the two almost overlapping impressions of the animal's trilobed metatarsal and metacarpal pads. The rear foot was placed nearly on top of the front track.

Tracks with Pads

Hundreds of species that you might find yourself tracking, from mice to moose, leave tracks comprising various, frequently confusing combinations and patterns of toe and larger pad prints. You'll be ahead of the game if you learn the basic types of prints left by different mammal families.

Probably the most common differentiation you will have to make when tracking is between canids and felids—the dog and cat families. These are common, mid- to large-size animals in many places, so their tracks are frequently encountered. Both show four toes and a single large pad, and their shapes and sizes can overlap enough to be confusing.

The diagrams below illustrate the salient differences between an idealized canid and felid track. It's vital to remember that only rarely will all or even most of these features be apparent in one track. Identification involves adding up as many characteristics as you can confirm before jumping to a conclusion—and often with blurred tracks there will simply be no firm conclusion! Don't let this discourage you; it is better to leave a track unidentified than to misidentify one. Note that we preface most descriptions with "tend to," as things are rarely as clear in the field as they are in a nice tidy illustration.

Here are several characteristics of canid tracks versus felid tracks:

- Canid tracks tend to be symmetrical and somewhat longer than wide—the simplest shape to fit around a canid track is usually a rectangle. If you draw a line across the toes perpendicular to the line of travel, the two front toes will be even with each other, as will the two rear toes.

- The two rear and outermost toes in canids generally point outward, and can be almost triangular in shape.

- The rear of the metacarpal or metatarsal pad in a canid normally displays two lobes, and the front of the pad displays one lobe.

- Canid tracks sometimes show claw marks, but this is a poor diagnostic for wild animals, as their claws tend to be worn down more than domestic dogs.

- You can often draw an X shape between the toes and the big pad in the track of a canid. In actual tracks this space frequently raises an X-shaped ridge of dirt, which can sometimes be spotted before the rest of the track becomes clear. (As a mnemonic, remember "X marks the spot, and Spot is a dog.")

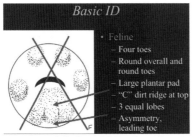
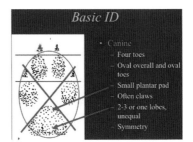

Diagrams of idealized felid and canid tracks.

Felid tracks retain similar characteristics no matter where you are. These African lion tracks (adult and cub) show the same three-lobed and asymmetrical pattern as a North American cougar—or your house cat.

- Felid tracks tend to be asymmetrical, showing a leading toe (like your own hand), and are roughly as wide as they are long—the simplest shape to fit around a felid track is a square or circle. If you draw a line perpendicular to the line of travel across the toes, they will not be even with each other.

- The rear of a felid metacarpal or metatarsal pad very often displays three distinct lobes. The front of the pad usually shows two lobes.

- You cannot draw an X between the toes and the big pad on a felid track. The space between the pads often pushes up a C-shaped ridge of dirt—and C of course stands for Cat.

- Felid tracks normally do not show claw marks, but they can under certain circumstances, such as when the animal is sprinting or climbing.

These characteristics are surprisingly uniform in canids ranging from tiny desert foxes to arctic wolves and in felids from bobcats to African lions (not to mention domestic dogs and cats).

Bears have paws that differ markedly from canids or felids. Bear tracks typically show five toes, and the rear track has a very long pad, sometimes almost human-like. Interestingly, the outermost toes on a bear's feet are larger than the inside toes.

Other, smaller animals you might find yourself tracking include members of the families Mustelidae (weasels, otters, badgers, wolverines), Mephitidae (skunks), Procyonidae (raccoons, coatis, and ringtails), Leporidae (rabbits and hares)—and even Rodentia (mice and rats). You'll find characteristics for each in the species accounts.

Hooved Tracks

Since the keratinized material of hooves is significantly harder than the relatively soft flesh of a pad, hooved animals usually make tracks that are more distinct in a given substrate. And since there is less variation among hooved animals, identification is made a bit simpler. Essentially you just need to determine if the print is from a single hoof (Perisodactyla) or a double hoof (Artiodactyla), and then proceed directly to shape and measurements to determine the species. Be cautious regarding potential double registers: Hooved animals such as deer, elk, and so on are food for many predators, and survival depends on remaining unnoticed. So when walking they will frequently place their rear hooves in the prints made by the front, to reduce noise. This makes measurement difficult, as the print can appear slightly longer than normal.

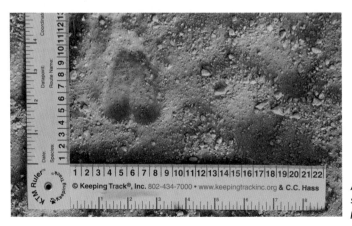

A white-tailed deer track shows up well in fine pulverized dirt in a road.

Other Tracks

Of course many other animals besides mammals, from insects to birds to lizards and snakes, make tracks as well. Bird tracks are easy to discern as they are bipedal and don't have any sort of broad pad. Their claw prints can be anisodactyl (three pointing forward and one backward), tridactyl (three pointing forward and none backward), zygodactyl (two pointing forward and two backward—see greater roadrunner), or didactyl (two pointing forward only, as in ostriches).

Snakes, of course, make one long track as they glide over the ground. The track can be straight when the snake is using a form of locomotion known as caterpillaring,

What would you make of these? The large round impression is where a rattlesnake coiled to wait for prey. The second photo shows the snake's track approaching and then later leaving the spot where it was coiled.

You can tell from the way the dirt is pushed up in the S pattern that this snake was moving from right to left.

or S-shaped if it is weaving back and forth to get traction. You can often tell which direction a snake was moving by looking for the earth pushed up in a ridge as the snake pushes back against it. Sidewinder rattlesnakes and a few other species can also move by lifting part of their body off the ground and looping it forward, creating a confusing set of disconnected S-shaped tracks. Lizards often leave a long track like a snake as their tails drag on the ground, except that there will be claw marks on either side.

Lizards normally leave a track that includes a tail drag mark.

Scat

There is, of course, another semi-durable sign that animals leave behind in their travels. However, unlike a perfect, clear footprint, scat (feces) is rarely reliable as an ironclad indication of species, unless it can be subjected to a DNA test. There are general characteristics associated with different species, to be sure, but—as we like to ask students: "Does *yours* always look exactly the same?"

Still, now and then scat serves as an additional piece of evidence to identify a track—or, more often, you might positively identify a set of tracks and then find some scat that fits the general characteristics for that animal.

As with their tracks, canids and felids tend to leave scat that exhibits unique traits. In general, for example, canid scat sections will have pointed tips (again making students squirm, we refer to this as a "DQ tip"), while felids leave blunt-tipped scat that shows regular constrictions or segments. (Ready? Think of a Tootsie Roll . . .) Scat from bobcats, lynxes, and mountain lions is usually dark and obviously nearly all animal in origin if you poke it apart with a stick—often bits of bone and teeth are present, along with a lot of hair. Coyote scat, on the other hand, might be nearly all animal, nothing but half-digested seeds, or a mixture. In the Southwest in summer, coyotes feed heavily on prickly pear cactus fruit, which is a deep red and leaves their

It's difficult to determine species with certainty from scat, but it can be an additional piece of evidence. What characteristics listed in the text would you say this matches?

scat noticeably dyed. Coyotes love to poop on the center lines of roads (either a territorial statement or a bit of nose-thumbing at humans, who can be sure?), and you can spot the bright magenta piles from a hundred yards off as you drive along.

Wild hooved animals tend to leave scat in neat oblong pellets, the size varying with the size of the animal. Rabbits and hares excrete pellets as well, but they are almost round rather than oblong.

Raptors (hawks, falcons, eagles, and owls) tend to leave long white streaks down the sides of their favorite roosting places (called "hawk chalk" by our falconer friends); however, after devouring a rodent or other prey item, the bones and hair are regurgitated in a pellet that can look remarkably like scat.

Reptiles do not have separate openings for voiding feces and urine; a single orifice called the cloaca serves both purposes. As a result, reptile scat usually has a white blob at the tip—this is nitrogenous waste that would be excreted as urine in mammals.

More advanced tracking books, such as the Peterson Field Guide's excellent work by Olaus Murie, include charts showing representative scat from many animals. Remember that it is only representative, however.

Key to Tracks by Size and Shape

The following key will help you identify quickly the animal tracks discussed in this book, and will give you an idea of how to proceed when evaluating any track. The first step is to determine its approximate size. This will tell you where to look in the key. Then judge its general shape: Is it round? Oblong? Is it a hoof, or does it show toes? Use the key to identify likely animals, then turn to the pages in this book where these animals' tracks are described and illustrated.

It's important to remember that these are very general size and shape guidelines; sizes vary widely between the sexes as well as from region to region and in different substrates (the type and condition of the dirt: mud, dry dust, rocky dirt, sand, and so on). Shape can also vary depending on the substrate and even on the speed the animal was traveling when it made the track. And don't forget that there will be an occasional anomaly. For three years we tracked a female mountain lion that had an extreme extension of the third toe on both of her front feet—these toes stuck out way above the others, and so she made a very odd track, much more oblong than the usual rounded cat print.

In the following key the letter F refers to the front foot; H refers to the hind foot.

Under ½ inch (1 cm)

Round

Four Toes*	Deer mouse F (p. 31)
Five Toes*	Deer mouse H (p. 31)

½ inch to 1½ inches (1 to 4 cm)

Round

Four Toes*	Eastern chipmunk F (p. 33); Longtail weasel (p. 49); Gray fox (p. 69)
Five Toes*	Eastern chipmunk H (p. 33); Striped skunk F (p. 45); Longtail weasel (p. 49); Badger H (p. 51); Ringtail (p. 63); Eastern gray squirrel (p. 35)
Indistinct Toes	Eastern cottontail F (p. 55)

Oblong or Rectangular   Ord kangaroo rat (p. 37); Striped skunk H (p. 45); Western spotted skunk (p. 47)

Hoof   Javelina (p. 77)

1½ inches to 3 inches (4 to 8 cm)

Round

Four Toes*	Coyote (p. 65); Bobcat (p. 71)
Indistinct Toes	Blacktail jackrabbit F (p. 57)

Oblong or Rectangular   Woodchuck (p. 41); Porcupine (p. 43); Eastern cottontail H (p. 55); Raccoon (p. 61); Badger F (p. 51); Virginia opossum (p. 59)

Hoof   White-tailed deer (p. 79); Pronghorn (p. 85)

Bird   Ruffed grouse (p. 23); Greater roadrunner (p. 25); Northern bobwhite quail (p. 21)

3 inches to 5 inches or more (8 to 13 cm)

Round

Four Toes*	Gray wolf (p. 67); Mountain lion (p. 75); Canada lynx (p. 73)

Oblong or Rectangular   Beaver (p. 39); Blacktail jackrabbit H (p. 57); Raccoon (p. 61); Black bear (p. 87); Wolverine (p. 53)

Hoof   Elk (p. 81); Moose (p. 83)

Bird   Great blue heron (p. 27); Common raven (p. 29)

*Most of the time this is true, but sometimes, depending on the substrate, one digit does not print, so a track that usually has five toes may show only four.

River banks are excellent places to find tracks, such as these from a raccoon.

3 Animal Tracks

In this chapter we describe and illustrate a variety of tracks made by common and interesting North American mammals and birds. The following information is provided for each animal:

Name: We have tried to list the most widely used common name for each animal, but where there's more than one, the others are mentioned in the text. We also list the scientific name, using the binomial system of genus and species; scientists occasionally change these names as they learn more about a species' genetic history.

Family: This is the scientific classification of the animal, which can be a useful clue to identification—sometimes animals in the same family leave similar tracks.

Size: The first size listed is the overall length of the animal itself. This is followed, when appropriate, by its tail length, height, and weight. These are very rough averages only—the size of individual animals varies greatly from region to region and between sexes. In general, northern animals are larger than southwestern animals, and males are bigger than females.

Habitat: Throughout North America there are many types of habitat, and we have used broad descriptions: desert, grassland, woodland, forest, and so on. This is the species' preferred place to live, but individuals may be found elsewhere.

Habits: A brief life history of the animal—its behavior, feeding preferences, and any other information that can be helpful to identification.

Tracking notes: These are tips for you on track identification, including information on similar species.

Birds (Aves)

NORTHERN BOBWHITE QUAIL

(Colinus virginianus)

Family Odontophoridae (New World Quail)

Size: 9¾ inches (25 cm) long

Habitat: Open woodlands and woodland edges, brushlands, farmlands, roadsides throughout the year

Habits: Like most quail, northern bobwhite quail eat seeds, leaves, and insects, foraging and roosting together in small flocks, or coveys, throughout most of the year. They break up into pairs during spring and summer for breeding. They are most active in the early morning and evening.

Tracking notes: There are five species of quail in the United States in addition to the bobwhite—the Montezuma quail (*Crytonyx montezumae*), scaled quail (*Callipepla squamata*), Gambel's quail (*Callipapla gambelii*), California quail (*Callipepla californica*), and mountain quail (*Oreortyx pictus*), all of the Southwest and West. Their tracks are nearly identical. Look for quail tracks in the mud around ponds or in the soft dirt of country roads in agricultural areas. Note that quail tracks are more delicate than grouse tracks (p. 23), and often are seen in quantity.

AT A GLANCE

1½ to 2 inches (3.8 to 5.1 cm)

Often in groups

Track substrate: mud

Habitat: pond edge

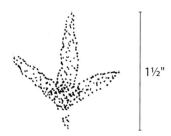

1½"

RUFFED GROUSE

(Bonasa umbellus)

Family Phasianidae (Partridges, Grouse, Turkeys)

Size: 17 inches (43 cm) long

Habitat: Deciduous and mixed woodlands throughout the year

Habits: In spring and summer these birds feed mainly on the ground for seeds, berries, flowers, leaves, and insects (sometimes small reptiles). In winter they feed up in trees, on buds.

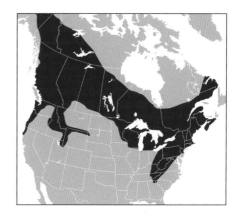

Tracking notes: There are seven species of grouse and prairie chickens in the United States—spruce grouse (*Dendragapus canadensis*) and sharp-tailed grouse (*Tympanuchus phasianellus*) of the North, blue grouse (*D. obscurus*) and sage grouse (*Centrocercus urophasianus*) of the West, and greater and lesser prairie chickens (*Tympanuchus cupido* and *T. pallidicinctus*) of the plains. Their tracks are similar. Look for grouse tracks around dense thickets of berry bushes or, in winter, beneath deciduous trees. Grouse tracks are more robust with wider-splayed toes than quail.

AT A GLANCE

2 to 2½ inches (5.1 to 6.4 cm)

Track substrate: mud

Habitat: pond edge

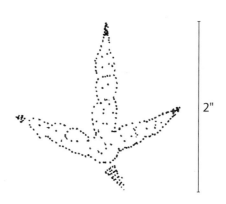

2"

GREATER ROADRUNNER

(Geococcyx californianus)

Family Cuculidae (Cuckoos)

Size: 23 inches (58 cm) long

Habitat: Desert, brushlands with open country throughout the year

Habits: Like the cartoon character, wild roadrunners do often run down or across roads, rarely flying except to glide short distances. They chase down insects, rodents, reptiles, and birds. Pairs mate for life.

Tracking notes: The track is a distinctive elongated X, with two toes forward and two back, a pattern called zygodactyl. When a roadrunner is running, its tracks are about 10 to 12 inches (25 to 30 cm) apart; when walking, about 3 to 4 inches (8 to 10 cm) apart.

AT A GLANCE

3 inches (7.6 cm)

X (zygodactyl) configuration

Track substrate: sand

Habitat: desert thornscrub

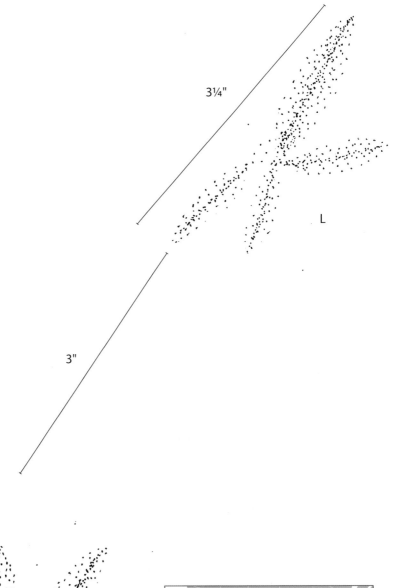

3¼"

3"

L

R

GREAT BLUE HERON

(Ardea herodias)

Family Ardeidae (Herons, Bitterns)

Size: 46 inches (117 cm) long

Habitat: Shores, marshes, swamps, tidal flats, ponds, creeks; year-round in central latitudes, but some move to northern regions of the range in summer and to southern regions in winter.

Habits: Great blue herons hunt by stalking around in shallow water, spearing fish, amphibians, and reptiles; near water, they will even eat birds and rodents.

Tracking notes: The track trail is often nearly in a straight line. Note the asymmetrical front toes and very long rear toe, typical only of the heron family. This increases stability while standing on one leg (as herons often do). Other heron tracks are smaller; only the great egret (*Ardea alba*) is of similar size.

AT A GLANCE

6 to 8 inches (15.2 to 20.3 cm)

Asymmetrical toes

Track substrate: mud

Habitat: tidal flat

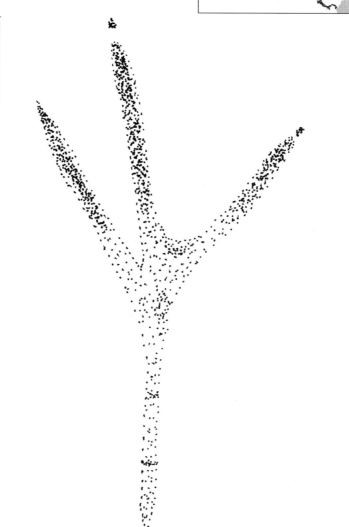

6"

COMMON RAVEN

(Corvus corax)

Family Corvidae (Crows and Allies)

Size: 25 inches (64 cm) long, including tail; around 2.5 pounds (1.1 kg)

Habitat: Deserts to plains to mountains

Habits: Ravens are among the most intelligent of birds, and have shown themselves capable of solving intricate puzzles in scientific tests. They also seem to know how to have fun; if you don't believe this, just search YouTube for "Ravens sliding in snow." Ravens are found over much of the western United States and across Canada, Europe, and northern Asia. They are omnivorous and will feed on berries and fruit, invertebrates, small birds and mammals, and eggs, as well as carrion and human garbage. In Yellowstone National Park, ravens quickly learned to follow reintroduced gray wolves to scavenge their kills. Ravens are distinguished from crows by their larger size and Roman-nosed beaks; they also rarely congregate

except at a large food source (although young birds can form small flocks). Ravens are very long-lived—captive individuals have lived forty years; lifespan in the wild is up to twenty years. They also tend to mate for life, and will return to the same nest year after year.

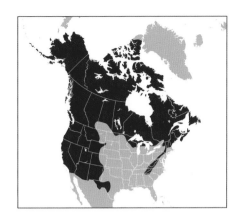

Tracking notes: Ravens sometimes walk with one foot in front of the other; at other times they'll hop and plant both feet nearly side by side. The middle toe of each foot usually points toward the inside of the line of travel.

AT A GLANCE

2¾ to 3¼ inches (7.0 to 8.3 cm)

Middle toes typically point inward

Track substrate: dirt

Habitat: desert thornscrub

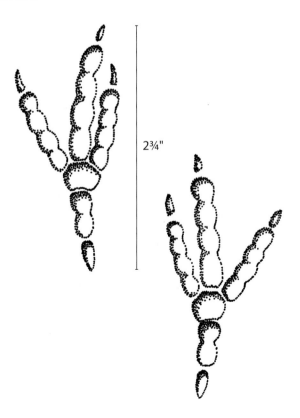

2¾"

Rodents (Rodentia)

DEER MOUSE

(Peromyscus maniculatus)

Family Cricetidae (Mice, Rats, Lemmings, and Voles)

Size: 2⅘ to 4 inches (7 to 10 cm) long, with a tail 2 to 5 inches (5 to 13 cm) long

Habitat: Nearly all habitats: deserts, grasslands, mixed woodlands, forests, towns

Habits: Primarily nocturnal, this omnivore (seeds, nuts, acorns, insects) is active all year. Deer mice set up house in underground burrows and holes in stumps, trees, and buildings—they are excellent climbers.

Tracking notes: Nearly all mice leave similar footprints; depending on the substrate, the pads, toes, and claws often register as groups of dots. Note the

pattern the feet make: The trail pattern, which might be called the gait, is nearly paired hind feet, with front feet slightly offset. This is typical of mice and chipmunks. Shrew tracks are similar, but generally the trail pattern of shrews is more closely spaced, and shrews tend to shuffle along. Also, mice eat seeds, leaving hulls behind, while shrews are carnivores.

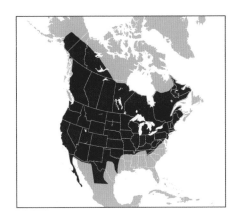

AT A GLANCE

⅜ to ½ inch (1 to 1.3 cm)

Five toes H, four toes F

Track substrate: mud

Habitat: garden

Typical gait

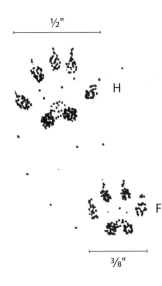

EASTERN CHIPMUNK

(Tamias striatus)

Family Sciuridae (Squirrels and Allies)

Size: 5 to 6 inches (13 to 15 cm) long, with a tail 3 to 4 inches (8 to 10 cm) long

Habitat: Deciduous forests and brushlands

Habits: Chipmunks are adaptable rodents that eat seeds, fruits, bulbs, insects, and eggs; they often store their food in holes underground. They are solitary—except females with young—and defend their feeding territories. There are at least sixteen

species of chipmunks in North America. Ground squirrels are similar in size and habit, but lack stripes on their face.

Tracking notes: The trail pattern is distinctive, as is the way four toes typically register on the front foot, five toes on the rear. Ground squirrel tracks are very difficult to distinguish from those of chipmunks.

AT A GLANCE

½ to ¾ inch (1.3 to 1.9 cm)

Five toes H, four toes F

Track substrate: wet sand

Habitat: creek-side brush

Typical gait

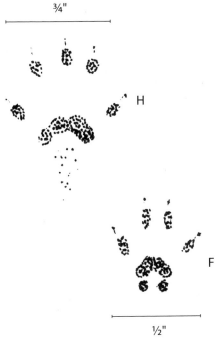

¾"

H

½"

F

EASTERN GRAY SQUIRREL

(Sciurus carolinensus)

Family Sciuridae (Squirrels and Allies)

Size: 16 to 20 inches (41 to 51 cm) long, including tail;
15 to 20 ounces (425 to 567 g)

Habitat: Dense, mostly deciduous woodlands, yards, city parks

Habits: One of the most ubiquitous mammals in the eastern United States, the gray squirrel seems as much at home in the wilderness as in the middle of Central Park (or in England, where it is an invasive species and has replaced the native red squirrel in many areas). In the wild, gray squirrels collect nuts and hoard them in scattered buried caches, and will create false caches to confuse potential rivals. In cities, gray squirrels bedevil homeowners who put out bird feeders, as they will make stupendous and comical gymnastic efforts to gain access to the contents. Gray squirrels nest in old woodpecker cavities in tree trunks or will build a nest of

leaves, which frequently remain visible in winter when the rest of the tree's leaves have fallen.

Tracking notes: Gray squirrel tracks typically show four toes on the front feet and five on the rear. In snow or soft ground, the front feet will sometimes show extra carpal pad prints. When bounding, the longer rear tracks are just ahead and outside of the front tracks.

AT A GLANCE

Front track at top

1¼ to 2 inches (3.2 to 5.1 cm)

Track substrate: loamy soil

Habitat: deciduous forest

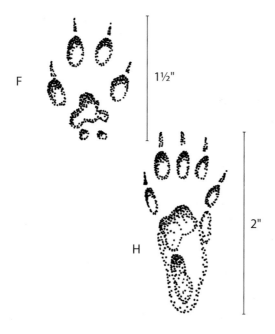

F

1½"

H

2"

ORD KANGAROO RAT

(Dipodomys ordi)

Family Heteromyidae (Pocket Mice and Kangaroo Rats)

Size: 4 to 4½ inches (10 to 11 cm) long, with a tail 5 to 6 inches (13 to 15 cm) long

Habitat: Deserts and desert grasslands

Habits: Kangaroo rats, nocturnal residents of arid and semiarid lands in the western United States, are so well adapted to dry conditions that they can get all their water needs from their food. They are so named because they have large, powerful hind legs on which they hop at high speeds or stand upright to forage, but despite the name, they are mice, not rats. Kangaroo rats gather seeds and store them in chambers in extensive underground burrows, which may have many access holes

and are topped by large mounds of earth up to 3 feet (1 m) high and 10 feet (3 m) wide. There are at least twelve species.

Tracking notes: Kangaroo rat tracks are distinctive: When an animal is foraging slowly, the long, triangular hind-foot heel shows clearly, as does the dragging of the long tail. When it's hopping quickly, tracks may not register clearly. Some species have four hind toes, some have five. The front feet rarely register clearly. Little mounds and depressions in the dirt indicate digging for buried seeds. Look for these tracks on sandy roads in arid lands (look to the sides of the road) or around their burrows; shallow depressions near holes may be dust "bathtubs."

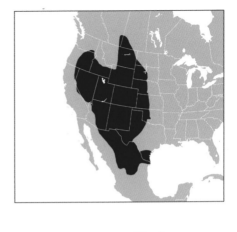

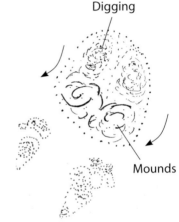

Digging

Mounds

AT A GLANCE

1 to 2 inches (2.5 to 5.1 cm) H

3- to 4-inch (7.6 to 10.2 cm) tail drag common

Track substrate: dust

Habitat: arid grassland

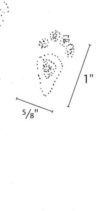

1"

5/8"

3½"

BEAVER

(Castor canadensis)

Family Castoridae (Beavers)

Size: 25 to 30 inches (64 to 76 cm) long, with a tail about 9 to 10 inches (23 to 25 cm) long; 40 to 60 pounds (18 to 27 kg)

Habitat: Streams, lakes, ponds with trees on or near banks

Habits: This largest of our North American rodents is nocturnal in much of its wide range, preferring to gnaw at night on the bark and small twigs of trees such as alder, aspen, poplar, birch, maple, willow, and cottonwood. Pairs and family members build dams across streams to create deep, slow water under which to build their living quarters, or lodges. Some populations build dens in streambanks instead.

Tracking notes: Look for the distinctive web-footed hind-foot tracks of beavers in the mud near their dams and lodges, though perfect tracks are hard to find, since

the heavy, paddle-shaped tail drags over the tracks. River otter tracks are smaller, usually show in two-by-two bounding hops, and often do not indicate the hind-foot web. Other beaver sign includes cut (felled) trees and peeled logs and twigs, with tooth marks from ⅛ to ¼ inch (3.2 to 6.4 mm) wide, and scent "signposts"—mud or mud-and-debris piles on which the beaver leaves territory-marking scent from special glands.

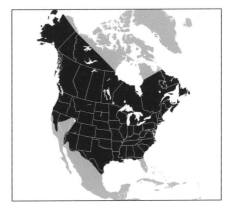

AT A GLANCE

6 to 6½ inches (15.2 to 16.5 cm) H

Track substrate: mud

Habitat: river

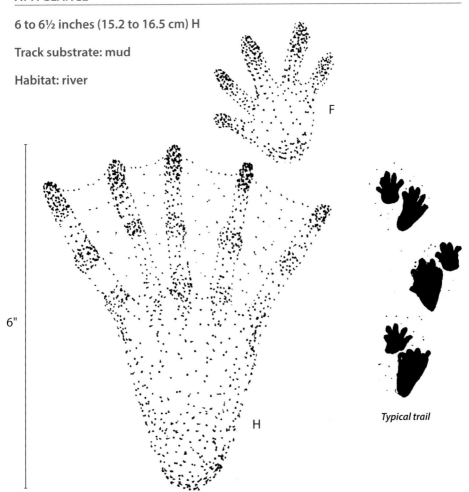

Typical trail

WOODCHUCK

(Marmota monax)

Family Sciuridae (Squirrels and Allies)

Size: 16 to 20 inches (41 to 51 cm) long, with a tail 4 to 7 inches (10 to 18 cm) long; 15 to 20 pounds (7 to 9 kg)

Habitat: Woodlands (especially rocky and brushy areas) and ravines

Habits: Large squirrels common in the woodlands of the eastern United States and much of Canada, woodchucks eat mostly succulent plant material. They forage during the day around their burrows, which are usually located in open meadows or meadow edges, especially near rocks or logs. Woodchucks hibernate in winter.

Tracking notes: The closely related yellowbelly marmot (*Marmota flaviventris*) lives in the western United States, mostly in the Rocky Mountains, Cascades, and Sierra Nevadas, while the hoary marmot (*M. caligata*) lives in Alaska, British Columbia, Washington, and Idaho. Woodchuck and marmot tracks are nearly identical. Typically, four toes register of the front foot and five of the hind foot, much like the tracks of their squirrel and chipmunk relatives. Sometimes the rear heel does not imprint, causing the rear track to appear smaller than the front one. When the woodchuck is walking, the hind foot often double registers in the front-foot track; when it's running, the track trail is similar to that of chipmunks and squirrels.

Raccoon tracks can appear similar, but the front-foot track of a raccoon shows five toes.

AT A GLANCE

1½ to 2 inches (3.8 to 5.1 cm) F

2 to 2¼ inches (5.1 to 5.7 cm) H

Track substrate: dry dirt

Habitat: woodland, rocky ravine

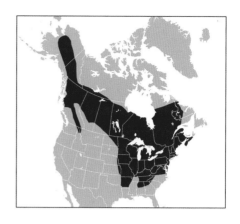

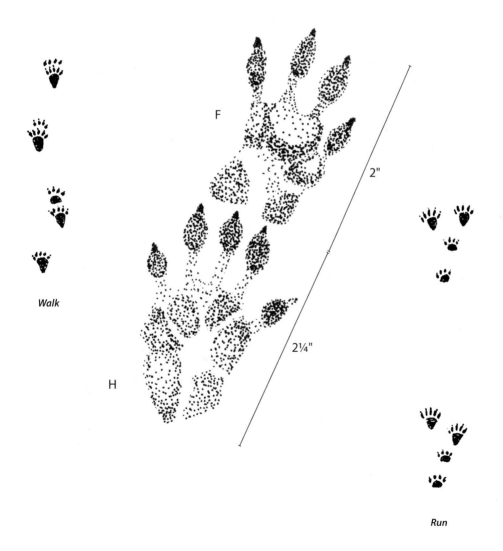

F

2"

2¼"

H

Walk

Run

PORCUPINE

(Erethizon dorsatum)

Family Erethizontidae (Porcupines)

Size: 18 to 22 inches (46 to 56 cm) long, with a tail 7 to 9 inches (18 to 23 cm) long; 10 to 25 pounds (5 to 11 kg)

Habitat: Woodlands and forests, occasionally shrublands

Habits: Porcupines are heavy and clumsy, and prefer to climb, however awkwardly, in the relative safety of trees as they munch buds, twigs, and inner bark. Most often

nocturnal, porcupines are also solitary, although there have been reports that they form small social groups in winter. During the day they sleep in hollow logs or dens and rock crevices. They mate in fall, when the usually quiet males grunt, groan, and broadcast high-pitched calls.

Tracking notes: Porcupine feet are unique, with large, callused pads; the waddling gait shows as toed-in tracks, but the dragging tail and spines often obscure much of the track trail, as if someone walked along dragging a broom. Look in and below trees for gnawed branches, bark, and twigs.

AT A GLANCE

2³⁄₈ to 2 inches (6.0 to 5.1 cm) H

Track substrate: damp dirt (back road)

Habitat: woodland

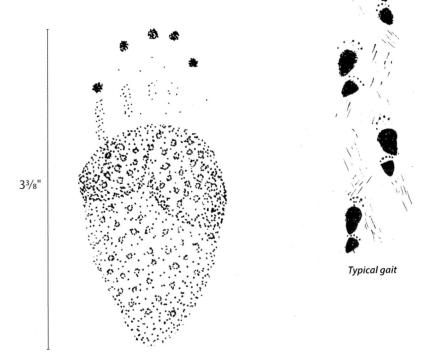

3³⁄₈"

Typical gait

Skunks (Mephitidae)

STRIPED SKUNK

(Mephitis mephitis)

Family Mephitidae (Skunks and Allies)

Size: 13 to 18 inches (33 to 46 cm) long, with a tail 7 to 10 inches (18 to 25 cm) long; 6 to 14 pounds (3 to 6 kg)

Habitat: Mixed woodlands and semi-open country

Habits: There are four species of skunks in North America, and all of them are voracious omnivores—they'll eat anything from meat to seeds to grubs to carrion—and although they prefer nocturnal activity, they will forage during the daytime. The striped skunk is the most widespread and commonly seen species. Although usually solitary, females will den together in winter (they do not hibernate). Natural densities are one skunk per 10 acres (4 ha), but numbers are much higher around campgrounds and suburban or cabin communities.

Tracking notes: The striped skunk is the most widespread of the four species and has nearly the largest tracks; the spotted skunk (*Spilogale putorius*) is also widespread but is diminutive, only 9 to 13 inches (23 to 33 cm) long; the hognose skunk (*Conepatus leuconotus*) is slightly larger than the striped, but like the slightly

smaller hooded skunk (*Mephitis macroura*), it is a southwestern species. The smaller track of the spotted skunk is easy to distinguish from the others by its small size, the frequent lack of a heel depression, and its darting, active track trail. Striped skunks move more deliberately and, being heavier, more often leave a full heel track.

AT A GLANCE

1 to 1½ inches (2.5 to 3.8 cm) F

1½ to 1⅞ inches (3.8 to 4.8 cm) H

Track substrate: moist dirt (creek-side trail)

Habitat: woodland

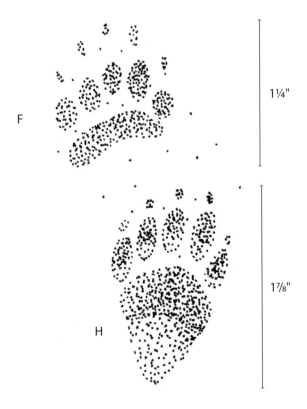

F

1¼"

H

1⅞"

WESTERN SPOTTED SKUNK

(Spilogale gracilus)

Family Mephitidae (Skunks and Allies)

Size: 15 to 18 inches (38 to 46 cm) including tail; less than 1 pound (0.5 kg) (females) to 2 pounds (1 kg) (males)

Habitat: Lowlands to about 7,000 feet; vegetated, rocky areas; often near streams

Habits: The tiny western spotted skunk (and its almost identical relative, the eastern spotted skunk), is about the size of a squirrel: We once watched one

disappear into a hiking boot, turn around inside it, and reemerge head first. Together the two species range nearly all the way across the United States. Spotted skunks are omnivorous, but feed mostly on animals, from insects and other invertebrates to mice, birds, and lizards. Spotted skunks are noted for their comical threat display, which sometimes involves a "handstand" on

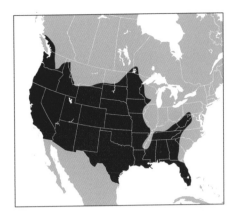

their front legs while the tail waves back and forth. Of course things stop being comical if the threat is ignored, as they can spray accurately up to 10 feet.

Tracking notes: Like all skunks, spotted skunk tracks normally show five toes front and rear, but they are tiny even in comparison to other skunks. In good tracking soil the complex rear metatarsal and tarsal pad prints almost look like six individual toe prints.

AT A GLANCE

Front track at top

⅞ to 1 inch (2.2 to 2.5 cm)

Track substrate: stream edge

Habitat: riparian woodland

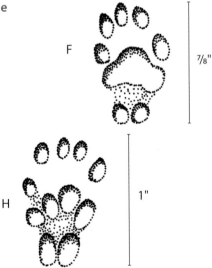

F

⅞"

H

1"

Mustelids (Mustelidae)

LONGTAIL WEASEL

(Mustela frenata)

Family Mustelidae (Weasels and Allies)

Size: 8 to 10½ inches (20 to 27 cm) long, with a tail about 3 to 6 inches (8 to 15 cm) long; 3 to 12 ounces (85 to 340 g)

Habitat: Nearly all habitats with access to water

Habits: Although widespread, the secretive weasel is rarely seen because its preferred time to hunt is at night. Small but fierce, longtail weasels eat rodents and even rabbits, as well as birds and reptiles. Most often they hunt along the water's edge—creeks, ponds, and lakes. They are solitary, and seek shelter and make their nests in burrows dug by other animals. Like all their relatives in the mustelid family, they have very aromatic scent glands. In winter most longtail weasels molt their brown pelts into white, which is valuable to trappers (southwestern weasels are not known to have white winter coats).

Tracking notes: The least weasel (*Mustela rixosa*) and the shorttail weasel (*M. erminea*) live mostly in the northern United States and Canada, with the shorttail's range extending south into California, Nevada, Utah, and Colorado. Look for weasel tracks—and the tracks of the related marten (*Martes americana*), mink (*Mustela vison*), and fisher (*Martes pennanti*)—along creeks

and the edges of ponds, where the animals like to hunt. They leave rounded tracks like cats, but the main pad often does not print completely, nor do all five toes (four is more common). In snow, weasel tracks are characteristically twinned, indicating a bounding gait. Except for the tracks of the fisher, which are 2 to 2¼ inches (5 to 6 cm) long, the tracks of the other weasels and their kin are very difficult to distinguish.

AT A GLANCE

1 to 1½ inches (2.5 to 3.8 cm) F

1½ to 1¾ inches (3.8 to 4.4 cm) H

Track substrate: moist dirt (creek-side trail)

Habitat: woodland

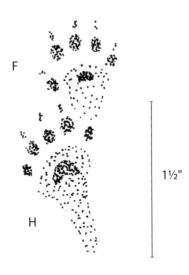

F

H

1½"

BADGER

(Taxidea taxus)

Family Mustelidae (Weasels and Allies)

Size: 18 to 22 inches (46 to 56 cm) long, with a tail 4 to 6 inches (10 to 15 cm) long; 13 to 25 pounds (6 to 11 kg)

Habitat: Deserts and grasslands

Habits: Badgers are surprisingly fierce for their squat, wide-bodied size; one was known to attack the tire of a truck that it felt was violating its territory. They hunt rodents by digging furiously with long, hooked claws until their prey is uncovered and caught. Although mostly active at night, they will venture out in cool mornings or late afternoons. Naturalists have observed coyotes and badgers cooperating on a hunt, or at least taking advantage of each other: While a badger digs for a rodent, the coyote sits at one of the rodent's other escape holes to snatch it up when it runs out—but sometimes the presence of the coyote causes the rodent to hold tight, allowing the badger to grab it. Badgers dig their own large burrows in embankments or slopes, usually shaded by a shrub or tree.

Tracking notes: Badger tracks are distinctly toed-in, and at least some of the long claws usually show. Sign of badger foraging includes lots of energetically dug holes, often with big rocks pulled out; like their relatives the skunks, they tend to dig along favorite paths or roadside berms. Badger den holes are shaped like badgers: wider than they are tall, about 8 inches (20 cm) high and 12 inches (30 cm) wide.

AT A GLANCE

1¾ to 2 inches (4.4 to 5.1 cm) F

1¼ to 1½ inches (3.2 to 3.8 cm) H

Tracks toed-in; front feet are larger

Track substrate: moist dirt (roadside puddle edge)

Habitat: desert grassland

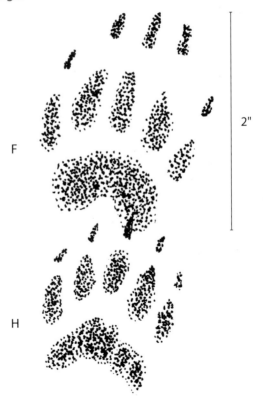

F

H

2"

WOLVERINE

(Gulo gulo)

Family Mustelidae (Weasels and Allies)

Size: 32 to 50 inches (81 to 127 cm) long, including tail; 23 to (rarely) 65 pounds (10 to 29 kg); males average about 45 to 50 pounds (20 to 23 kg)

Habitat: Remote, forested mountain ranges of the northern United States and Canada

Habits: The wolverine is the largest terrestrial member of the weasel family (only the sea otter is bigger), and its reputation for fierceness outmatches its size: They've been known to take down mule deer, caribou, even elk and moose. They also feed on carrion, and will drive larger predators off kills. Wolverines have dense fur and large paws that enable them to negotiate deep snow easily, and huge claws useful for climbing trees and steep cliffs. The range of wolverines in the United States has diminished drastically. Today they are known only in the Cascades in Washington and in the Rockies of Montana, Wyoming, and Idaho, but there are signs the population might be stabilizing and even expanding. Still, a wolverine track is a lucky find.

Tracking notes: Wolverine tracks usually show five toes on both front and back feet, and in addition to the metacarpal pad there is sometimes a small extra carpal pad print present, especially in snow. The common trail of a wolverine is peculiar and diagnostic: a series of three tracks one after the other, slightly offset in a diagonal pattern.

AT A GLANCE

Front track at top (tarsal pad does not always print)

5½ to 7¼ inches (14 to 18.4 cm) F

4½ to 5¼ inches (11.4 to 13.3 cm) H

Track substrate: light snow

Habitat: evergreen forest

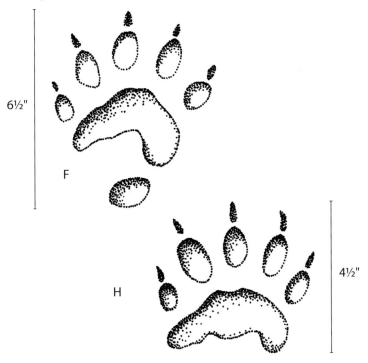

6½"

F

H

4½"

Rabbits and Hares (Leporidae)

EASTERN COTTONTAIL

(Sylvilagus floridanus)

Family Leporidae (Hares and Rabbits)

Size: 14 to 17 inches (35 to 43 cm) long; 2 to 4 pounds (1 to 2 kg)

Habitat: Brushy and weedy areas, meadow and forest edges

Habits: The common "bunny rabbits" in most of the Midwest and East as well as northern Mexico, eastern cottontails are active mostly from the early evening until the late morning. During the warmer parts of the day, they rest in little depressions in the dirt called forms, in their burrows, or in the deep shade of dense shrubs or brush piles. In spring and summer, cottontails eat grasses or forbs; in winter, twigs and bark.

Tracking notes: There are four other species of closely related (and difficult to differentiate) cottontails in the United States and Mexico: desert (*Sylvilagus auduboni*), mountain (*S. nuttalli*), New England (*S. transitionalis*), and brush (*S. bachmani*). The swamp (*S. aquaticus*) and marsh rabbits (*S. palustris*) are unique in their wetland habitats. The four cottontails leave nearly identical tracks, usually without distinct pads and toe markings—two elongated rear feet and two round

front feet, often with the rear feet placed before the front; swamp and marsh rabbits leave more distinct toe and pad marks. Cottontails leave conspicuous rabbit-sized dust-bath depressions, with scratch marks and sometimes droppings, near their burrows and favorite foraging areas. Jackrabbit tracks are larger—2½ inches (6 cm) and up to 5 inches (13 cm) in snow for hind feet—

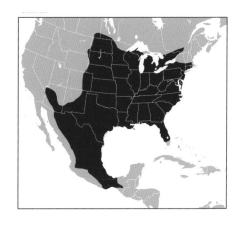

and the distance between track groups is greater.

AT A GLANCE

2 to 3½ inches (5.1 to 8.9 cm) H

1 to 1⅜ inches (2.5 to 3.5 cm) F

Track size varies, especially hind feet

Track substrate: dust (back road)

Habitat: woodland

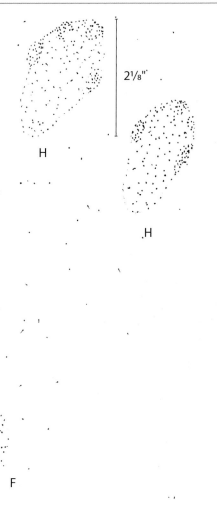

BLACKTAIL JACKRABBIT

(Lepus californicus)

Family Leporidae (Hares and Rabbits)

Size: 17 to 21 inches (43 to 53 cm) long; 3 to 7 pounds (1.4 to 3 kg)

Habitat: Grasslands and deserts

Habits: Like its little relative the cottontail, the blacktail jackrabbit is active from the early evening through the morning, retiring a little earlier than the cottontail. Blacktails browse on forbs and grasses and rest in dense shade during the day; they do not have dens. Jackrabbits are tall and often move with a loping walk rather than hopping, though they do hop—sometimes as far as 10 feet (3 m) per hop when traveling fast, which they do, up to 35 mph (56 km/h).

Tracking notes: The track pattern is highly variable: When they're walking, blacktails leave tracks that can look similar to coyote, and when they're hopping quickly, the track sets can be very far apart and thus hard to follow. To help you distinguish, look for the classic rabbit pattern of paired hind feet placed in front of the front feet. Dirt roads in deserts and grasslands are good places to find jackrabbit tracks. Tracks of the whitetail jackrabbit (*Lepus townsendi*) of the plains, the antelope jackrabbit (*L. alleni*) of the Southwest and Mexico, and the European hare (*L. europaeus*) introduced in the East are nearly identical to those of the

blacktail; the range and habitat of the animals can help you distinguish species.

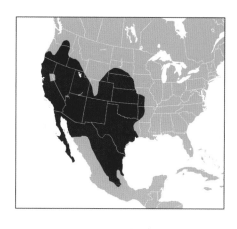

AT A GLANCE

4 to 6 inches (10.2 to 15.2 cm) H

1½ to 2 inches (3.8 to 5.1 cm) F

Track size varies, especially hind feet; hops or walks

Track substrate: sand

Habitat: desert

H

5"

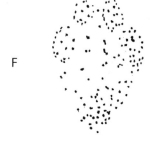

F

Marsupials (Didelphidae)

VIRGINIA OPOSSUM

(Didelphis virginiana)

Family Didelphidae

Size: 22 to 50 inches (56 to 127 cm) long, including tail (opossums have one of the largest size ranges of any single species of mammal); males, 1.8 to 13 pounds (0.8 to 6 kg); females, 12 ounces (0.4 kg) to 8 pounds (3.6 kg)

Habitat: Widely spread: forests, farmland, urban edges

Habits: The only marsupial found in the United States, the opposum is a member of a primitive mammalian line whose most famous members are the kangaroos and wallabies of Australia. However, contrary to what you might think, marsupials spread from the Americas to Australia, not the other way around, when the continents were still joined. As a marsupial, opposums give birth to very undeveloped young, which then move to a pouch to suckle and complete their growth. Opossums have prehensile tails that can grasp tree limbs or small objects, and fifty teeth— the most of any North American mammal. Opossums are slow and lack serious defenses, and are thus preyed upon by numerous other mammals and birds of prey; to counteract this mortality, they can breed up to three times per

year and raise thirteen young at a time. They are omnivorous and will eat plant matter, invertebrates, and small reptiles and mammals.

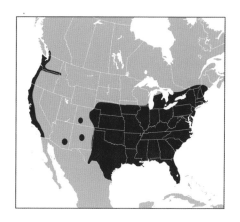

Tracking notes: Opossums leave startlingly distinctive tracks due to the opposable "thumbs" on their rear feet: They stand out at more than 90 degrees from the other toes, making them hard to mistake for any other animal. Opossums show five toes on both front and rear feet.

AT A GLANCE

Front track at top

2 to 2.5 inches (5.1 to 6.4 cm)

Note "opposable thumb" on rear foot

Track substrate: dirt road

Habitat: riparian canyon

F

2"

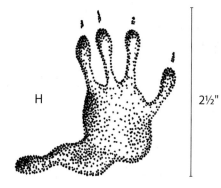

H

2½"

Procyonids (Procyonidae)

RACCOON

(Procyon lotor)

Family Procyonidae (Raccoons and Allies)

Size: 18 to 28 inches (46 to 71 cm) long, with a tail 8 to 12 inches (20 to 30 cm) long; 12 to 35 pounds (5 to 16 kg)

Habitat: Near wetlands, waterways, bodies of water, and oceans, especially with adjacent woodlands or rocky outcrops

Habits: The ubiquitous masked raccoon well deserves its reputation as a clever troublemaker. Raccoons are omnivorous—they'll eat anything from fruit and nuts, to invertebrates, frogs, and fish, to garbage and dog food in suburban areas—and they have powerful and dexterous front paws with which they crack open crayfish or pry open garbage cans and climb trees or porch posts. They use dens in rock crevices, underground holes, or tree or log hollows to raise their young or spend cold periods in winter, although they do not hibernate.

Tracking notes: Raccoons leave distinctive tracks when their toes print: The front foot looks like a miniature human hand, with five long fingers; the hind foot is similar to the human foot, with five long toes, but the heel and foot pad is diamond shaped and elongated. Look for raccoon tracks in mud alongside creeks, lakes, or the ocean; their foraging is evident in discarded

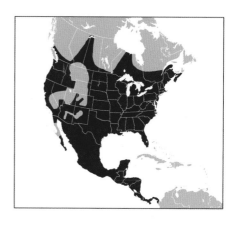

bits of animal carcasses. Raccoons have two relatives in North America, the coati (*Nasua narica*) and the ringtail (*Bassariscus astutus*). Coatis live in mountain canyons of Mexico, southern Arizona, and New Mexico, and often travel in large troops; their tracks are similar to those of raccoons but lack the elongated toes. Ringtails are more solitary, live in chaparral and canyon country, are very small—2 pounds (1 kg)—and leave tiny, catlike tracks.

AT A GLANCE

2 to 4 inches (5.1 to 10.2 cm) H

Bulbous toes show, looks like human hand; hind is larger

Track substrate: mud

Habitat: mountain canyon (Southwest)

Typical gait

2¼"

RINGTAIL

(Bassariscus astutus)

Family Procyonidae (Raccoons and Allies)

Size: 24 to 30 inches (61 to 76 cm) long, including tail, which is as long as the body; 1.5 to 3 pounds (0.7 to 1.4 kg)

Habitat: Rocky canyons, riparian corridors, caves

Habits: Sometimes incorrectly referred to as a ringtail cat, ringtails were also called miner's cats because of their affinity for caves and mine tunnels, and their propensity for becoming quite tame (and controlling mouse infestations). One thing that isn't in question is their startling black-and-white-ringed tail, which is

huge in relation to the animal's slender 2-pound (1 kg) body. Found throughout the southwestern United States except in the driest deserts, ringtails are opportunistic feeders, eating anything from berries and cactus fruit to invertebrates, small mammals, and reptiles. Their large ears and eyes are adapted for a nocturnal existence.

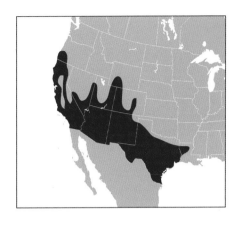

Tracking notes: A ringtail's hind feet can rotate 180 degrees to make descending trees or bluffs easy. We watched one disappear in what seemed a suicide move over a sheer cliff at the Grand Canyon; a cautious look over the edge revealed the ringtail effortlessly clinging to the rock upside down. Like other procyonids, ringtail tracks show five toes front and rear. The front tracks often show extra carpal pad prints as well.

AT A GLANCE

1 to 1½ inches (2.5 to 3.8 cm)

Track substrate: dirt yard

Habitat: desert thornscrub hills

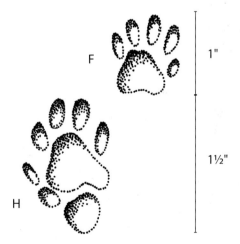

F

1"

H

1½"

Dogs (Canidae)

COYOTE

(Canis latrans)

Family Canidae (Dogs, Wolves, and Allies)

Size: 32 to 37 inches (81 to 94 cm) long, with a tail 11 to 16 inches (28 to 41 cm) long; 20 to 50 pounds (9 to 23 kg)

Habitat: Most habitats in North America

Habits: One of the emblematic animals of the American West, the coyote actually lives from Alaska south into Mexico, and is expanding into eastern and northeastern states. Coyotes are not uncommon in most cities within their range. One reason they are so successful is that they eat anything from plant matter to carrion, and everything in between; they will kill deer and sheep and calves, usually working in a team or pack. Housecats are a favorite prey in urban areas. Although largely nocturnal, they are active whenever prey is active, and for coyotes that's anytime. They dig dens into embankments, well hidden by brush.

Tracking notes: Coyotes will cruise up to 10 miles (16 km) or so on a foraging expedition, and they will often take the easiest route, such as a dirt road or trail—look for their small, delicate tracks (like a flower) trotting straight down the middle. You can also look for the telltale "diagonal trot" common to wild dogs (although they do not always make this pattern): Wild and some domestic dogs will trot with their body at a

diagonal aspect to their line of travel, so that the tracks of the front feet land on one side of the track trail, while those of the hind feet land on the other (see illustration). Claws don't always show. Like many mammals, coyotes increase in size (and likewise their tracks are larger) in northern latitudes. Domestic dog tracks are "messier" (the toes often splay much more than a coyote's), and they do

not tend to trot purposefully down the middle of trails; instead they wander hither and yon. Fox tracks are smaller and barely leave pad and toe marks. Wolf tracks are much larger and robust.

AT A GLANCE

Front track at top (front feet are larger to support weight of the head)

2¼ to 2¾ inches (5.7 to 7.0 cm) F

2 to 2⅜ inches (5.1 to 6.0 cm) H

Front is larger; sometimes double registers and trots diagonally

Track substrate: mud

Habitat: southwestern forest

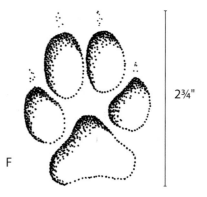

2¾"

F

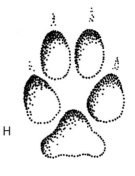

H

GRAY WOLF

(Canis lupus)

Family Canidae (Dogs, Wolves, and Allies)

Size: 43 to 48 inches (102 to 122 cm) long, with a tail 12 to 20 inches (30 to 51 cm) long; 70 to 120 pounds (32 to 54 kg)

Habitat: Forests and tundra

Habits: The gray wolf, also called the timber wolf, is one of the last great—but now rare—predators of North America, its haunting howl an icon of wilderness. Forming packs of up to twelve or more individuals during the nonbreeding season, wolves hunt big game, such as caribou and deer, as well as elk, sheep, and small cattle. They also eat rodents and other small mammals and birds, and are not known to attack people. Like coyotes, they are active whenever their prey is moving around, night or day, and they cover great distances when hunting, often using favorite trails. Wolves dig dens in embankments or rocky outcrops, where they are protected but also able to see danger approaching.

Tracking notes: Wolf tracks, like those of their relatives the coyotes and foxes, are distinctly rectangular—longer than they are wide (rather than quite round, like cats' tracks). Look for the diagonal trot (see Tracking notes for the coyote, p. 64), and look for tracks along trails in areas where wolves are known to hunt. Claws show more often than in coyotes. Wolf dens are much larger than coyote dens. In Arizona, New Mexico, and northern Mexico, the Mexican wolf (*Canis lupus baileyi*) was once a much more common predator, but by the middle of the twentieth century

the species was all but extinct. By the beginning of 2000, several packs had been reintroduced in the Blue Range Wilderness of Arizona, on the New Mexico border, and some Mexican biologists think a few wild wolves might survive in their country. Mexican wolves are slightly smaller bodied than gray wolves of the North.

AT A GLANCE

4¼ to 4¾ inches (10.9 to 12.1 cm) F

3¾ to 4½ inches (9.5 to 11.4 cm) H

Front is larger; same gaits as other canines; toes splay more than coyote

Track substrate: mud

Habitat: forest

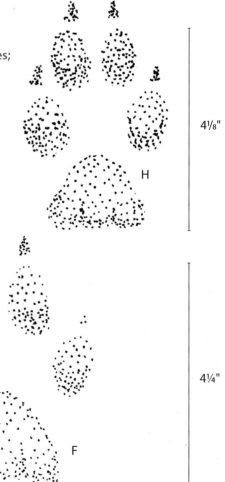

4⅛"

H

4¼"

F

GRAY FOX

(Urocyon cinereoargenteus)

Family Canidae (Dogs, Wolves, and Allies)

Size: 21 to 29 inches (53 to 74 cm) long, with a tail 11 to 16 inches (28 to 41 cm) long; 7 to 13 pounds (3 to 6 kg)

Habitat: Oak and deciduous woodlands, mountain canyons, chaparral, high deserts

Habits: The gray fox is a very unusual canine, for it has semiretractable claws and readily climbs trees to eat bird eggs and nestlings. Gray foxes also eat small mammals, insects, fruits, and nuts. Nocturnal hunters, gray foxes are very secretive and thus rarely seen, except perhaps darting across backcountry roads. They den in hollow logs or in holes in rocky outcrops or embankments.

Tracking notes: The gray fox is smaller than its bushy coat and tail advertise; weighing about as much as a housecat, they barely leave discernible tracks except in mud. Their rear-foot tracks often lack the complete main pad—just a small oval, the center. Claws rarely show. Look for their tracks along roads or around canyon creeks. The even smaller kit or swift foxes (*Vulpes velox*) of the western United States and northern Mexico leave similar tracks to those of the gray fox, but usually (not

always) slightly smaller, and usually in more arid and open-country habitats. The red fox (*V. vulpes*) is widespread in North America; its tracks are usually distinct from those of other foxes in that its feet are furred on the bottom, making fuzzy tracks, and if the main pad prints, it usually shows a distinctive raised horizontal ridge (like a bar) across the pad.

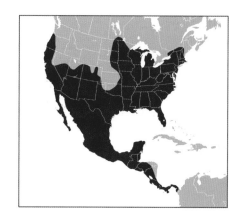

AT A GLANCE

1¼ to 2 inches (3.2 to 5.1 cm) F

1 to 1½ inches (2.5 to 3.8 cm) H

Front is larger; same gaits as other canines; rear pad often barely registers

Track substrate: dust

Habitat: desert grassland/canyon mouth

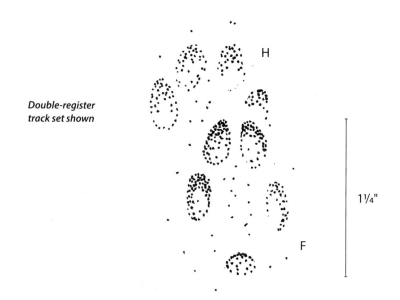

H

Double-register track set shown

1¼"

F

Cats (Felidae)

BOBCAT

(Felis rufus)

Family Felidae (Cats and Allies)

Size: 25 to 30 inches (64 to 76 cm) long, with a 5-inch (13 cm) tail; 15 to 35 pounds (7 to 16 kg)

Habitat: Forests, woodlands, canyonlands, deserts

Habits: Bobcats are very adaptable and have become increasingly common in suburban areas within their habitats. Although primarily nocturnal, they will hunt in the early morning or late afternoon for preferred prey such as rabbits and birds (especially in suburban areas, where bird feeders provide convenient snack bars). They make their dens in hollows of logs or under rocks.

Tracking notes: Bobcats prefer the cover of thickets and woodlands rather than open trails, so when they travel—which they do for 25 to 50 miles (40 to 80 km) within their hunting range—they do not often leave noticeable track sets like the wild dogs that trot for great distances down trails or roads. Look for bobcat tracks crossing roads or trails, but rarely walking down them for appreciable distances. Although superficially similar in size to their canine counterparts (bobcat/coyote; mountain lion/wolf), feline tracks are rounder in overall shape than canine, with proportionally more main pad showing (more often showing a three-lobed base of the main

pad) and rounder toe pads (oval in dogs). Mustelid tracks usually show five toes, cats (and dogs) four. Bobcat tracks are smaller than mountain lion tracks, although a large male bobcat's track might be close to that of a young lion, especially female. Lynx (*Lynx canadensis*) tracks show fur between the wide-spread toes, obscuring the pads.

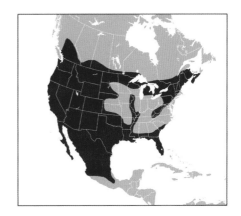

AT A GLANCE

1½ to 1¾ inches (3.8 to 4.4 cm) H

1¾ to 2 inches (4.4 to 5.1 cm) F

Front is larger; note roundness of toes and overall track

Track substrate: dust

Habitat: mountain canyon

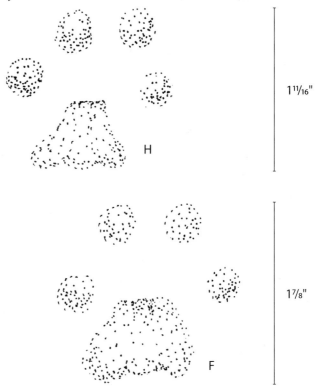

H

1^{11}/$_{16}$"

F

1^{7}/$_{8}$"

CANADA LYNX

(Lynx canadensis)

Family Felidae (Cats and Allies)

Size: 30 to 40 inches (76 to 102 cm) long, about 20 inches (51 cm) tall at the shoulder; 19 to 25 pounds (9 to 11 kg)

Habitat: Northern boreal forests

Habits: This slightly larger close relative of the bobcat looks even larger than it is thanks to its luxurious, thick fur and gigantic paws that act as snowshoes in deep winter powder. The lynx is further distinguished by the long black tufts on its ears, a ruff with black points on either side of its chin, and did we mention those huge paws? The Canada lynx is a predator that has evolved to prey heavily on one species: the snowshoe hare, which matches the lynx for deep-snow prowess. The

lynx hunts by ambush and a short chase; if it is not successful within a few yards it generally breaks off. Historically, lynx and snowshoe hare populations follow each other through dramatic up and down cycles.

Tracking notes: The lynx shows all the normal field markings of felid tracks—asymmetry, three-lobed metacarpal and metatarsal pads, etc.—but its heavily furred feet can obscure individual characteristics—in fact, in heavy snow it's sometimes difficult to differentiate the tracks of a lynx from those of its snowshoe hare prey.

AT A GLANCE

Front track at top

3½ inches (8.9 cm)

Tracking substrate: snow

Habitat: boreal forest

F   3½"

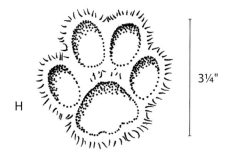

H   3¼"

MOUNTAIN LION

(Felis concolor)

Family Felidae (Cats and Allies)

Size: 42 to 54 inches (107 to 137 cm) long, with a tail 30 to 36 inches (76 to 91 cm) long; 80 to 200 pounds (36 to 91 kg)

Habitat: Mountain forests and woodlands

Habits: Rarely seen, mountain lions nonetheless thrive in most of the mountains of the American West, western Canada, and Mexico. Also called pumas and cougars, they are expanding into the eastern United States. Their ranges are closely tied to the presence of plentiful deer, mostly the whitetail, but they do eat smaller mammals, cattle, and sheep. Where humans have encroached on their habitat and diminished their prey, instances of humans attacked by lions have increased. Lions' home ranges are large—100 square miles (259 sq km) or so for males, less for females—and they move widely in these ranges; 20 miles (32 km) a night is not uncommon.

Tracking notes: See Tracking notes for the bobcat (p. 70) for information on distinguishing feline and canine tracks. Unlike their smaller relative the bobcat, lions will walk for long distances down back roads and trails. When stalking, they will (like other predators) double register (see chapter 2), but when they walk at cruising speed, all four feet will register separately. Lions use their feet to make scrapes (p. 92)—piles of dirt or leaves on which they urinate or defecate as scent

markers, or "signposts," for delineating territory or communicating mating availability to other lions. After they make a kill, lions drag their prey to thick cover and may eat just a portion of it (often the main organs) before partially burying the rest, returning several days in a row until it is gone (p. 93). In lion country look for their tracks and scrapes on back roads and trails (scrapes will be beside trails), and keep your eye out for drag marks of prey.

AT A GLANCE

Male track shown

3 to 3¾ inches (7.6 to 9.5 cm) F

2¾ to 3 inches (7.0 to 7.6 cm) H

Front is larger; note roundness of toes and overall track

Track substrate: dry dirt (back road)

Habitat: mountain canyon

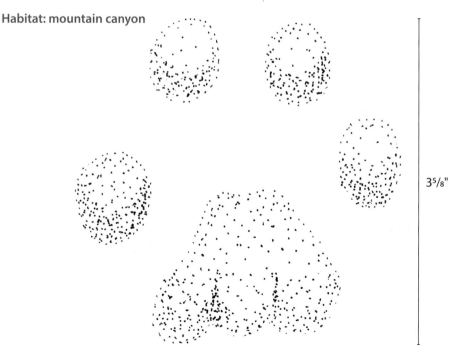

3⁵/₈"

Hoofed Animals (Tayassuidae, Cervidae, Antilocapridae)

JAVELINA

(Tayassu tajacu)

Family Tayassuidae (Peccaries)

Size: 34 to 36 inches (86 to 91 cm) long; 40 to 50 pounds (18 to 23 kg)

Habitat: Deserts and semidesert shrublands

Habits: Called javelina (haav-a-LEE-na) or peccaries, these common wild "pigs" of the Southwest and Mexico patrol their territories in groups of several to perhaps twenty-five if food is plentiful. From the late afternoon through the early morning, they forage for seeds, fruits, cactus pads, grubs, bird eggs, and invertebrates. They breed throughout the year, and so you might see little rust-colored spotted young

(called reds) anytime, but be careful: Javelina are fiercely protective of their herd and have long, sharp canines.

Tracking notes: Javelina tracks can be distinguished from deer by their blunt tips—the track looks like two human thumbprints pressed side by side into the dirt. Look for them around water holes, near creeks, and, in suburban areas, around bird feeders.

AT A GLANCE

Note characteristic blunt tips to hooves

1¼ to 1½ inches (3.2 to 3.8 cm) F

1 to 1⅜ inches (2.5 to 3.5 cm) H

Front is larger; often in herds

Track substrate: dry dirt

Habitat: upland desert

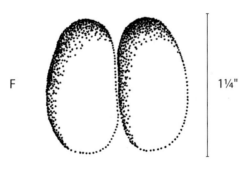

F   1¼"

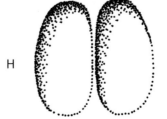

H

WHITE-TAILED DEER

(Odocoileus virginianus)

Family Cervidae (Deer and Allies)

Size: 3 to 3½ feet tall (91 to 107 cm); males, 75 to 400 pounds (34 to 181 kg); females, 50 to 250 pounds (23 to 113 kg)

Habitat: Forests and woodlands

Habits: The most widespread deer in North America, the whitetail is best known for its wide, short tail with a white underside, which it holds up like a flag when alarmed (hence its other name, flagtail). Whitetails browse forbs and new grasses, leaves, twigs, fungi, and acorns. In fall and winter bucks gather up large herds, or "harems," of females in preparation for the rut, or breeding season, using their antlers to fight each other for dominance. In summer females stay in groups of two or three, usually mothers and last year's offspring, or young-of-the-year.

Tracking notes: The Coues' whitetail (*Odocoileus virginianus cousei*), an acknowledged subspecies found in the Southwest and Mexico, is the smallest form of whitetail. Distinguishing whitetail tracks from those of the mule deer (*O. hemionus*), a western desert and grassland species, is difficult if not impossible because their sizes overlap, but habitat can provide a clue (although when they

occur in the same area, they can mix at woodland-grassland edges). So can one trait: When running, whitetails gallop like horses and rabbits, planting their powerful hind feet far ahead of their front feet; mule deer bound, or "pogo," with all four feet striking the ground at once, an action called stotting or pronking. By late summer and fall, males' antlers have regrown (they drop off in

spring), and they scrape off the velvet covering by thrashing their antlers in trees; look for twisted, damaged, and tangled shrubs.

AT A GLANCE

2¾ to 3 inches (7.0 to 7.6 cm) F or H, eastern

1¾ to 2 inches (4.4 to 5.1 cm) F or H, southwestern (Coues')

Track substrate: dry dirt

Habitat: woodland

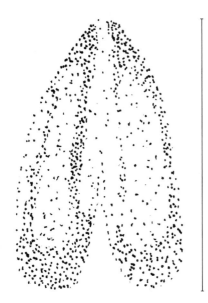

Double-register

2⁷⁄₈"

ELK

(Cervus canadensis)

Family Cervidae (Deer and Allies)

Size: 4 to 5 feet (122 to 152 cm) tall; males, 700 to 1,000 pounds (318 to 454 kg); females, 500 to 600 pounds (227 to 272 kg)

Habitat: Semi-open forests and woodlands, meadows

Habits: Also called wapiti, elk are majestic forest dwellers, foraging together in large breeding herds in winter—by breeding season the bulls have formed "harems" of females—and in summer, in small single-sex groups, usually females and young and old or young males together. During breeding season, the "rut," males do battle and bugle loudly as they vie for females. Elk browse huge quantities of forbs, grasses, twigs, and bark in the morning and early evening, and at night if the moon is bright. During winter they migrate down into the lower woodlands; in spring they head back to the high country.

Tracking notes: Elk tracks are much larger and rounder than deer tracks, but can be hard to distinguish from young cattle, with which they often share habitat; look around for adult cow tracks and droppings (although even elk pellets and young cow "pies" can be similar if they are eating similar foods). Moose tracks are usually longer, sharper, and more elongated than elk tracks, but they can also be very hard to differentiate for sure. In late summer male elk shed the velvet on their new racks and, like their relatives the deer, will rub them in shrubs

and trees to help the process; look for thrashed, tangled, and broken shrubs or small trees. In fall during the rut, bulls will wallow in mud puddles and ponds; sometimes they use the same ones each year. Elk (and moose) love to eat aspen bark, so look at elk-head height for spots of stripped-off bark and old black scars from years of gnawing.

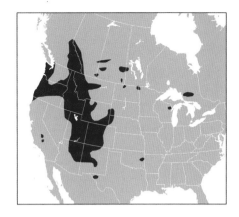

AT A GLANCE

3⁷⁄₈ to 4¾ (9.8 to 12.1 cm) F or H

Track substrate: dried mud

Habitat: southwestern forest

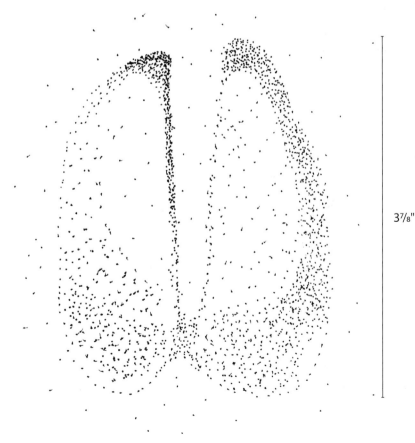

3⁷⁄₈"

MOOSE

(Alces alces)

Family Cervidae (Deer and Allies)

Size: 5 to 6½ feet (152 to 198 cm) tall; males, 850 to 1,180 pounds (386 to 535 kg); females, 600 to 800 pounds (272 to 363 kg)

Habitat: Forests, near bodies of water

Habits: The ungainly looking moose is actually a pretty fierce protector of its young and can move surprisingly fast if it wants to. Otherwise, moose spend most of their time browsing leisurely on aquatic vegetation—they don't hesitate to enter and stay in water for long periods—supplemented by forbs, twigs, bark, and saplings, especially willow but also aspen and other forest trees. Moose are strong swimmers, having been clocked at speeds up to 35 mph (56 km/h). They are solitary, and unlike their relatives the deer and elk, bulls do not form "harems" during the fall rut.

Tracking notes: See Tracking notes for elk (p. 80) for differentiating from moose. Moose foraging sign includes willows and saplings of other trees such as cottonwoods broken over at the tops, with the leaves stripped from the bent-over twigs, as well as trees such as fir and aspen being stripped of all low (as high up as a moose can reach) branches and twigs—as if a meticulous groundskeeper has been at work.

AT A GLANCE

4¼ to 5¼ inches (10.9 to 13.3 cm) F or H

Track substrate: mud

Habitat: forest wetland

5"

PRONGHORN

(Antilocapra americana)

Family Antilocapridae

Size: Males stand about 38 inches (97 cm) high at the shoulder; 75 to 135 pounds (34 to 61 kg)

Habitat: Open terrain and grasslands

Habits: The pronghorn, sometimes called antelope, can sprint at up to 55 mph (89 km/h) and run for hours at 30 mph (48 km/h). The only faster land mammal is the cheetah, and cheetahs have little endurance for long chases. Coincidence? Not at all: Cheetahs and pronghorns evolved together in North America during the Pleistocene epoch. With the former extinct on this side of the ocean, no predator stands a chance of running down a pronghorn; they are most vulnerable as calves, when coyotes and eagles prey on them. Surprisingly, despite their speed pronghorn are poor jumpers and will dive under a fence at full speed rather than

jump over it. Pronghorn are found in a broad swath of the plains states and in isolated pockets elsewhere in the West where open grassland flourishes. Adult males are generally solitary except during mating season (September); young males form herds, as do females.

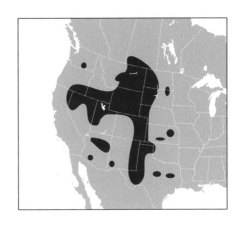

Tracking notes: Pronghorn tracks resemble white-tailed deer tracks in size, but the outer edges of pronghorn hoof prints are concave toward the front.

AT A GLANCE

2 to 3¼ inches (5 to 8.25 cm)

Track substrate: grass clearing

Habitat: grassland

F 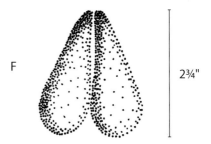 2¾"

H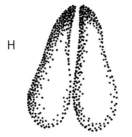

Bears (Ursidae)

BLACK BEAR

(Ursus americanus)

Family Ursidae (Bears)

Size: 5 to 6 feet (152 to 183 cm) long, 2 to 3 feet (61 to 91 cm) tall at shoulders; 200 to over 475 pounds (91 to over 215 kg)

Habitat: Forests and woodlands

Habits: Although one of our largest carnivores, the black bear actually eats mostly tubers, berries, nuts, and insects and their larvae, rounded out with deer, small mammals, eggs, carrion, and (unfortunately) garbage and pet food in suburban areas. It is in these areas where humans have encroached on bear habitat that bears have attacked people. Black bears are active mostly at night during spring and summer; in winter in most areas, they hibernate in dens.

Tracking notes: Bears follow favorite feeding routes in their territories and use the easiest thoroughfares, so look for their tracks along trails and roads; during summer look around fruiting shrubs especially, and look for torn-up old logs and turned-over rocks (where they have searched for insects). On bear feet the "big toe" is actually the outside toe (equivalent of the human pinkie toe). The round heel pad of the front foot often does not register, and in soft dirt the small inside toe (equivalent to the human big toe) often will not print, leaving a four-toed print. Bears also use trees: They bite off strips of bark to get at the sweet sap and will also rub against a favorite, sometimes biting and clawing it repeatedly, leaving it scarred. Grizzly bears (*Ursus arctos horribilis*) live in the northern United States, up into Canada and Alaska, in forest and tundra habitat. They are much larger than black bears—6 to 7 feet (183 to 213 cm) long and 325 to 850 pounds (147 to 386 kg)—and will

kill mammals as large as elk. However, they more often dig for rodents—marmots are a favorite—with their huge claws, and consume a great deal of fruit, grasses, insects, and fish. To tell grizzly tracks from those of black bears, draw a straight line from the bottom of the big toe across the top of the metatarsal pad of the front-foot track. If the line intersects the little toe in the middle or above, it is a black bear; if it intersects in the bottom half or not at all, it is a grizzly.

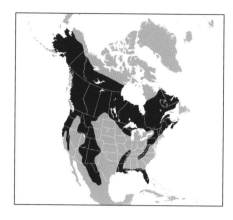

AT A GLANCE

4 to 4½ inches (10.2 to 11.4 cm) F

7 to 7½ inches (17.8 to 19.1 cm) H

Note that only four of five toes printed in this track

Track substrate: dry dirt (creek-side trail)

Habitat: mountain canyon (southwest)

4¼"

F

7"

H

4 Other Animal Signs

Dirt Mounds, Holes, and Runways

Animals make lots of other marks in the earth in addition to tracks. Mounds that have no holes are made by mole crickets, moles, voles, and pocket gophers. See the photos on pages 88–90 for some typical holes, and also see the individual animal listings in chapter 3 for more information on their holes. Runways are just what they sound like: dirt paths that are worn by animals as they travel the same foraging routes each day or night. You can see runways of ants, mice and kangaroo rats, cottontails, shrews, and even grizzly bears, which leave twin tracks worn down over the years in the tundra vegetation.

1. This hole (and those nearby) under a creosote bush were made by a single kangaroo rat. Multiple entrances give the rodent multiple escape routes should a snake enter one of them. Note the well-worn path where the animal enters and leaves.

2. Well hidden under a fallen log, this bobcat den, round and 8 inches (20 cm) in diameter, is just above a creek in a mountain canyon. The position allows the cat to assess its surroundings before entering or exiting its den. It's likely used only for giving birth to and rearing kittens, or for daytime resting.

3. Dug into the embankment of an old dry creek bed in grassland habitat, this coyote den is 15 inches (38 cm) high and 10 inches (25 cm) wide; it has been in use for several years. It is about 6 feet (183 cm) deep and 2 to 3 feet (61 to 91 cm) wide inside. Partially concealed by an overhanging tree and shrubs, it still affords good views of approaching danger.

4. A good generalization regarding burrows is that they will be no larger than necessary for the animal that made them. Desert tortoises dig burrows deep enough to protect them from frost in the winter. The shape is just like a tortoise: flat on the bottom and arched on top.

5. Female tarantulas make vertical holes in which they wait to ambush passing vertebrate prey. In the daytime they partially block the entrance with web. If you see a tarantula out wandering about, it is frequently a male in search of a female.

Scrapings, Scratchings, Drillings, and Gnawings

During the course of foraging, marking territory, mating, and rearing young, animals deliberately make marks on the ground or in trees and shrubs. Woodpeckers and sapsuckers drill holes in trees to look for insects, get at sap, or store nuts; sapsucker holes usually are in neat rows, while woodpecker holes are more random. Woodpeckers also excavate holes in trees in which to build their nests; the entrance holes are neat and round, just barely bigger than the bird. Rodents, from very small to large, chew on twigs and small branches, and on bones and discarded antlers. Wild dogs scratch out with their hind feet after scent marking (when they urinate) to better distribute the scent. For more animal signs, see the photos on the following pages.

1. There are always mysteries to be solved. These strange-looking marks were made by a coati, a raccoon-like animal of the Southwest. Coatis sweep their long, sensitive noses back and forth against the ground to sniff for burrowing invertebrates, and the results are these semicircular marks.

2. Mountain lions will scrape up a pile of dirt and debris and then urinate or defecate on top of it. This is a scent marker, a "sign-post," in or at the edge of their territory. It's a territorial claim that says, "This is mine." Lions use the same marking spots repeatedly; females will leave a special scent on males' sign-posts when they are ready to mate. The leaves in this photo are sycamore.

3. If you see a drag mark like this, look closely and you'll see deer or javelina hair scraped off on the rocks. If you follow it—not advisable!—you might find where the mountain lion has eaten part of its kill then partially buried the rest for a later meal.

4. This is a typical mountain lion kill, a whitetail deer, which has been dragged under cover and partially buried with debris. The lion will stay nearby to feed on the remains for up to a week.

5 Keeping Track of Your Tracks

One of the best ways to learn to identify tracks is to permanently enshrine the ones you find. The physical and mental act of photographing, drawing, or casting a track plants it that much more firmly in your brain's hard drive—and keeping a record of tracks reminds you of places visited and adventures enjoyed.

Photography

A photograph provides the most reliable record of a track, but it must be done properly to ensure complete accuracy. Almost any camera or smartphone will do, but setting up the shot is critical. The camera should be absolutely parallel with the substrate and directly above the track, to avoid distorting the appearance of the print. Holding the camera too close will also distort the image; you generally want to photograph from about 24 inches away.

A photo of a track without some reference for measurement loses much of its value. While in a pinch any object of known size will suffice, it's much more professional to use a two-sided tracking ruler such as seen in the photographs in this book. They're available from Keeping Track (www .keepingtrack.org). Use a dry erase marker or pencil to write the date and other

A proper track photograph should be taken from directly above the print, with a tracking ruler oriented along the direction of travel for scale. Note the slanting light and good contrast.

information about the track on the ruler. Generally, you want to place the base of the ruler at the back of the track, as close as possible without disturbing it, with the vertical side of the ruler along either side of the track. Since the best time to photograph tracks is also the best time to spot them—early morning or late afternoon when shadows are long and contrast is high—make sure the ruler does not cast a shadow into the track. Take several shots, and make sure you get a crisp focus. If the sun is high or contrast is otherwise poor, you can try the mirror or flashlight trick described in chapter 1.

If you don't have a ruler, any object of known size will do for scale when photographing a track. This set of keys shows the relative size of a bobcat print.

Tracing

A tracing of a track gives you an instant and accurate record that you can keep in a journal, and it's an excellent way to learn how to discern the true outline of a print. You'll need a small sheet of plexiglass, about 5 by 7 inches (unless you plan to trace grizzly bear tracks!), a fine-point dry erase marker, and blank white paper. First, suspend the plexiglass directly over the track, just an inch or so above it, using caution to avoid disturbing it. You can use four pebbles for this; if you'd rather carry something, wine corks are lightweight and a good height when laid on their side. With the dry erase marker, carefully outline the track on the plexiglass, making sure you are looking straight down and outlining the true track rather than the displaced material around it. Once you've finished, put a piece of paper over the plexiglass, hold it up to the sun or over another light source, and trace your tracing onto the paper. Then you can write down the pertinent information on the paper.

Plaster Casts

Making plaster casts could be the most fun you'll have tracking—kids, especially, become totally engrossed in it. And a cast of a cougar or coyote or bobcat print makes a fantastic conversation piece displayed on a bookshelf or coffee table.

Plaster of Paris is cheap and easy to find at most hardware stores. The larger 8-pound bucket will give you enough for years of casting, and stores easily. Here's the field kit we carry:

- Five or six strips of poster board cut about 2 inches wide and 12 to 20 inches long, rolled carefully together for storage in a plastic peanut butter jar (below)

- A few paper clips

- A freezer-weight gallon zip-top bag containing another zip-top bag with four to five cups of dry plaster

- A clean empty 12-ounce plastic peanut butter jar

- Two or three heavy-duty plastic spoons

- A few extra zip-top bags

- A stiff toothbrush

To make a cast, form one of the paper strips into a ring large enough to encompass the track with an inch or more to spare. Secure the paper strip with two paper clips and carefully place it around the track. Press the paper strip down, being careful not to disturb the track. Put a quantity of plaster into the empty jar (you'll have to learn the correct amounts by experience; about a cup does it for a small mammal track) and begin adding water and mixing with a spoon until the mixture is the consistency of pancake batter—not runny, but not so stiff that it won't pour.

Carefully pour the plaster into the track ring, but don't pour it right on the track—pour it off to the side of the track and let it flow in. Make sure it flows over the whole track and to the ring's edge, preferably about ¾ inch or more thick (the thicker it is, the stronger, but a thicker cast will take longer to cure). If you don't mix enough, just make sure the track is covered with the first batch, then mix more to fill in the edges and over the top. You don't have to use the ring (sometimes you can't because of uneven ground); in this case just make the plaster mixture a little thicker—it will stop flowing when you stop pouring.

Let the cast dry for about 30 minutes, then gently pry it up and place it in an extra bag to take home. Let it dry completely—overnight is best—then gently scrub the cast clean with a toothbrush under running water. Allow it to dry again and then label the back of the cast with permanent ink: species, location, habitat type, substrate type, and any other information you can gather, such as other nearby tracks, scat, and so forth.

Soot Station

You can make an effective sooted track trap from a cardboard box turned on its side, a margarine tub for bait glued far back to the rear, a sooted aluminum baking sheet (coat it with soot by holding it—with hot pads!—over a kerosene flame, a campfire, or any other dirty flame until it has an even, fairly thick coating) duct-taped to the entrance of the box, and a sheet of clean white paper taped to the box between the sooted sheet and the bait. Place the trap out overnight where you know there to be skunk, rodent, or raccoon activity; bait with peanut butter or rolled oats.

When the animal walks over the sooted sheet to get the bait, it makes its own track prints on the white paper. It's fun to check in the morning for mystery guests. As you would with other track-preserving methods, label the paper with as much information as you can. To keep the track from smearing, you can cover it with a sheet of laminating plastic, or apply a commercial spray fixative, available in art supply stores.

6 Conservation Projects

Animal tracking can be more than just a fun activity. Organized and well-documented track counts on selected roads, trails, or marked transects can be an excellent means not only of establishing the presence of large carnivores such as wolves, bears, or mountain lions but also of recording their critical habitat and favored routes as they move around feeding and breeding (large carnivores need lots of space just to eat). The data can subsequently be used to urge land managers to preserve existing open space, purchase land for a new preserve, or establish wildlife corridors between unconnected parks or forest preserves, as well as by whole communities to plan for future growth when they write community plans.

Scout groups, hiking clubs, hunter advocacy organizations, outdoor enthusiasts, and community planning groups can organize their own track counts. To gain the expertise necessary to spearhead a track count for conservation, several people from the organization should take a class in tracking for community activists (see appendix B for names and contact information). A successful track count should be held regularly—one of the country's most successful, in southern Arizona, occurs just once a year, but more often is better to hold interest for the group. Try monthly. Transects and road and trail routes should be assigned the night before the count so that teams—each with two or three people—can get an early start. Everyone heads out in the early morning armed with data recording sheets, clear rulers and calipers, cameras, and tracing or plaster kits for capturing really good tracks after they're photographed with a ruler. Groups return to camp after completing their assigned routes, and the afternoon is spent collating and discussing finds. Late afternoon routes may be run as well.

It's absolutely vital to maintain scientific integrity when conducting transects. It's natural to want to find tracks, but the lack of animal sign in a particular area is information equally as important as the presence of it. Likewise, identification should be conservative; no species should be recorded without firm photographic evidence.

To turn your data into action on behalf of wildlife, your group should work with a local land or wildlife management agency or a community growth-planning group (or all three). These groups can use the data to make decisions about habitat management and conservation. It takes many months or years of data collection, along with a lot of hard work, attention to detail, and persistence in the often-frustrating and convoluted public policy arena to see any rewards. But these rewards can be priceless: a legacy of land and wildlife preservation for future generations.

APPENDIX A: BASIC TRACKING KIT

You can enjoy tracking with no equipment at all except your eyes, but if you want to be as successful as possible, and especially if you want to keep a record of your findings, you'll want a kit comprising many of the things we've already discussed:

- Camera

- Folding tracking ruler

- Mirror

- Flashlight

- Plaster casting kit (see chapter 5)

- Tracing kit (see chapter 5)

- Notebook

- Binoculars (for spotting actual animals!)

- GPS unit (to record an accurate location)

- Local track guide or book

- Brimmed hat (surprisingly effective for reducing glare while looking for tracks)

- You can carry this kit in anything, but we like a shoulder-carry field bag, such as those made by Filson, to keep everything organized and convenient.

APPENDIX B:
ADDITIONAL RESOURCES

Books

Burt, William H., and Richard P. Grossenheider. *A Field Guide to the Mammals of America North of Mexico*. Peterson Field Guides, Houghton Mifflin, 1998. The best field guide to animal identification, range, and behavior.

Halfpenny, James. *A Field Guide to Mammal Tracking in North America*. Johnson Books, 1988. Excellent for technical details of print physiology and measurements. Halfpenny also has about a half dozen other fine books on regional tracks and scat in the western United States.

Murie, Olaus J. *Animal Tracks*. 2nd ed. Peterson Field Guides, Houghton Mifflin, 1998. The best natural history tracking book ever written, and perhaps ever to be written, by one of America's greatest naturalists.

The Smithsonian Book of North American Mammals. Smithsonian Institution Press, 1999. The most comprehensive, up-to-date resource on mammals of North America. For serious students of tracking and mammals.

Periodical

Earth Skills Newsletter. A quarterly publication of the Earth Skills school, this newsletter is worth its weight in gold for the information it provides students of tracking. It also contains information on early cultures and primitive skills. Highly recommended.

Schools and Classes

A Naturalist's World (P.O. Box 989, Gardiner, MT 59030). On-site field classes with James Halfpenny and Diann Thompson. They also maintain a useful website: www.tracknature.com.

Earth Skills (1113 Cougar Ct., Frazier Park, CA 93225; [661] 245-0128; www.earth skills.com). A nature and wilderness skills school that offers excellent beginning to advanced tracking classes in the West.

Keeping Track (P.O. Box 444, Huntington, VT 05462; [802] 434-7000; www .keepingtrack.org). A unique organization that teaches animal tracking to communities and groups interested in animal and habitat conservation.

The Tracker School, Inc. (P.O. Box 173, Asbury, NJ 08802; [908] 479-4681, Fax [908] 479-6867; www.trackerschool.com). Tom Brown Jr.'s tracking, nature, and wilderness survival school.

Other Resources

We work with a southwestern organization called Sky Island Alliance that has been organizing track counts for twenty years and has produced data used by state and federal governments and land agencies for planning and conservation. If you want to find out more about how they use tracking for conservation, contact Sky Island Alliance, P.O. Box 41165, Tucson, AZ 85717; (520) 624-7080; www.skyislandalliance.org.

The Bear Tracker's Den (www.bear-tracker.com) is an excellent website covering tracking, with lots of tracks, natural history information, pictures, sounds, animation, links, and resources and ideas for educators.

ABOUT THE AUTHORS

Award-winning authors and naturalists **Roseann** and **Jonathan Hanson** have worked as a team for thirty years, exploring and writing about the wilds of North and South America, Europe, and Africa. Jonathan and Roseann teach animal-tracking courses for nonprofit conservation groups. They live in Tucson, Arizona.